Chick Wit

Chick Wit

Over 1000 Humorous Quotes
from Modern Women

JASMINE BIRTLES

PRION

First published in Great Britain in 2004 by

Prion
an imprint of the
Carlton Publishing Group
20 Mortimer Street
London W1T 3JW

10 9 8 7 6 5 4 3 2

ISBN 1 85375 538 9

A catalogue record for this book is available from the
British Library

Typeset by e-type, Liverpool
Printed in Great Britain
by Mackays

Contents

SECTION FOUR: Body and Soul

SECTION FIVE: Sex and Other Laughing Matters

Acknowledgements

Big thanks to my 'glamorous assistant' Kerry 'Kezzer' McCarthy who did a load of good work on this book. Also thanks to my agent Darin Jewell for all his help, my editor Miranda West for great ideas and good direction and to friends who came up with quotes and ideas. Enjoy!

Introduction

To quote or not to quote ... that is the question ...

I always have a quotation for everything – it saves original thinking.

Dorothy L. Sayers

Everyone likes a good quote, and everyone loves to misquote. Such is life. But the joy of a good quote is that in just one sentence it can sum up a world of meaning and experience. If it can do it in a witty and entertaining way so much the better. That must be why books of quotations are so popular: the phrases are true,they make us think and they don't take up much time doing so.

But, let's be honest, a mere list of quotations, enjoyable though it is, has a limited value on its own. The quotes may be true, may be funny, may even be true and funny (many of the ones in this book certainly are) but what is the use of them? How can you use them, rather than just reading and smiling at them?

Introduction

Good question. Glad you asked. In fact, the point of this introduction is to initiate you, the reader, to the very art of using quotations: where to use them, how to use them, which to use and which simply to smile at in the comfort and privacy of your own boudoir. Think of it as the place where you can ask all the questions you wanted to ask about quotations but never thought it was worth bothering before.

Thank goodness, I have so many questions about quotations and I never even realised it!

Quite. And there are more like you. What would you like to ask first?

Well, firstly, what is the best way to deliver a quote in, say, one of those standing-up-balancing-a-glass-trying-to-be-entertaining-type-of-parties, and which are good ones to use?

It depends on the reaction you want to get. If you are bored to tears by the conversation and just want to jiggle things up a bit you could launch in with no preamble saying something like 'You know, I think it was Susan Sarandon who once said "You have to be careful not to be upstaged by your nipples" and I think she was so right. Don't you?' Or simply quote the writer Kathy Lette's line: 'Why

9

did the Aussie bloke cross the road? 'Cause his dick was in the chicken.' It's important to say it with a serious and even earnest face – no hint of humour – or it won't have the desired effect.

On the other hand, if you want to seem intellectual drop the right names. For example, you might casually remark that 'Lady Thatcher once said "In politics, if you want anything said, ask a man; if you want anything done, ask a woman" … or was it Britney Spears? I get them so muddled.'

Also, have a look at the list of top tips for delivering quotations in social situations at the end of this introduction.

Are there any quotations that are good for one situation and not for another?

Oh yes! For example, in the bedroom it could be a great idea to quote a few sex sirens like the wonderful Mae West 'To err is human but it feels divine.' Or Pamela Anderson who said 'I don't think about anything too much … If I think too much, it kind of freaks me out.' However, neither of those two sentences is an ideal comment to make in the boardroom or at a meeting with your bank manager. Of course, there are also some that shouldn't be used in either situation, such as this one from Ali Smith: 'Being a Scot and a lesbian are two big handy ticks next to my name right now,' or even Kim Catrall's 'You've no idea how many men I've had to sleep with to win this.'

If you're a mother having coffee with friends you could repeat Roseanne Barr's quip 'They're all mine … Of course, I'd trade any of them for a dishwasher', or Jo Brand's 'They say men can never experience the pain of childbirth … they can if you hit them in the goolies with a cricket bat … for fourteen hours.' But it's probably best not to air them when at tea with your mother-in-law.

Some quotes should be copied out and stuck on your fridge – 'Don't cook. Don't clean. No man will ever make love to a woman because she waxed the linoleum – "My God, the floor's immaculate. Lie down, you hot bitch."' (Joan Rivers, comedian); some stuck above your computer 'Always suspect any job men willingly vacate for a woman.' (Jill Tweedie); and some next to your mirror 'If you're so worried that you have to cut your face up to make yourself happier, you're with the wrong guy.' (Jerry Hall).

Speaking at your golden wedding anniversary you could raise some kindly laughs with Rita Rudner's line 'Before I met my husband, I'd never fallen in love, though I'd stepped in it a few times.' but probably not with Mamie Van Doren's 'I've married a few people I shouldn't have, but haven't we all?' unless you're really secure.

Introduction

So why have you only got quotations from women in this book – and only modern(ish) women, too?

To redress the balance. Look at books of quotations even from ten years ago and the words are overwhelmingly from men. Understandable, really, given that we still live very much in a man's world and they've had a good twenty centuries at least to think up some good lines. Also, it is still believed, by women as well as men, that women are just not witty – unless by accident – so it's useful to give them a whole book to themselves to prove them wrong.

Of course, there are, and have been, other books of quotes from women but you tend to see the same ones over and over again. Admittedly, it can be harder to find a truly witty quote – or even something half-intelligent – from some of the   stars of today (you know who you are, you pop and Hollywood divas) but they do exist. Bringing out a book of new and cool quotations (with some of the best from the last century too) will, I hope, encourage more of you, dear female readers, to come up with your own pithy lines of witty genius!

Well, if you're going to get serious, frankly, reading the quotes about men, marriage and relationships I'm now so depressed I wonder why we bother with any of them.

Good point and I'm glad you noticed it. Remember these are witty quotes and most are funny because they're true, but they're not the whole truth. That can be the problem with any comedy – it's often easier to be funny by pulling things and people down rather than building them up. Some men may be bastards but, honestly, not all of them are ... well, not all of the time, anyway.

Interestingly, many male comedians and comedy writers are miserable and difficult people and (in my experience, at any rate) can have deep personality problems with long medical names. In the main, this is not so true of the female of the variety, although there are some notable exceptions. Dorothy Parker, for all her genius, led somewhat of a loser's life, which probably fuelled her brilliant, biting satire (although one wonders which really comes first, the miserable life or the miserable attitude). More recently, the prolific British comedy writer Debbie Barham, who was turning out fabulous lines for TV, radio and print from her early teens onwards, sadly died of anorexia when she was just 27. You can see her line on eating disorders in the 'Food and Drink' section.

Comedy is regularly just the flip-side of tragedy and is often entered into by people who hold so much hurt and confusion inside that it is the only way they can make sense of the world. So don't take any of it too seriously!

Introduction

OK, so do you have any quick tips on delivering quotes in a social situation or somewhere where it really matters, like during a presentation for the Board of Directors?

Certainly – here are my Ten Top Tips for being thought a well-read, witty genius just by using quotations:

1. Go for short quotes – they're easier to remember and deliver.
2. Memorise a few clever, funny quotes that could be used in several different situations – it's less effort merely to repeat yourself.
3. Don't do those quote signs in the air with your fingers – it's just so '90s!
4. Try not to screw your face up or put on a silly voice to make it funnier.
5. Learn a few obscure but funny quotations, practise saying them, then pass them off as your own. Only sad quotation-collectors like me will notice.
6. Don't laugh before the punchline.
7. In fact, try not to laugh even after the punchline. If you have to laugh, it's not funny.
8. To look really intellectual, learn a witty French or Spanish quote or whatever language you can manage, quote it in the original then, as if you do it all the time, translate into English. Look around as if you expect everyone to know that quotation as well as you do.

9. Try to get it right. If you can't quite get it right, at least get it to make sense.

10. Probably best never to quote Jade Goodie (that's Jade-from-Big-Brother, if you were wondering) in any situation other than with irony. After all, who would willingly admit that they 'thought Cambridge was in London', wondered 'Am I minging?' believed 'East Angula is abroad' or that 'people in Portugal they speak Portuganese, don't they?' Mind you, it hasn't stopped her earning more than the average university graduate, so maybe ignorance really is bliss, or at least lucrative.

On the other hand, rather than dishing out these pearls to all and sundry, you could just keep them to yourself and do as Dorothy Parker suggests: 'I might repeat to myself slowly and soothingly, a list of quotations beautiful from minds profound – if I can remember any of the damn things.'

Yours quotingly

Jasmine Birtles

Being You!

Wisdom

Experience: A comb life gives you after you lose your hair.

Judith Stern, writer

Good judgement comes from experience, and often experience comes from bad judgement.

Rita Mae Brown, writer

Happy people are never brilliant. It implies friction.

Katherine Mansfield, writer

If life throws you a lemon – make lemonade.

Joan Collins, actor

Time is a dressmaker specialising in alterations.

Faith Baldwin, writer

Whatever you choose, however many roads you travel, I hope that you choose not to be a lady.

Nora Ephron, writer

Being You!

Always have a vivid imagination, for you never know when you might need it.

J.K. Rowling, writer

From birth to 18 a girl needs good parents; from 18 to 35, she needs good looks. From 35 to 55, good personality. From 55 on, she needs good cash. I'm saving my money.

Sophie Tucker, entertainer

Only a few things are really important.

Marie Dressler, actor

It's said in Hollywood that you should always forgive your enemies – because you never know when you'll have to work with them.

Lana Turner, actor

A friendship can weather most things and thrive in thin soil; but it needs a little mulch of letters and phone calls and small, silly presents every so often – just to save it from drying out completely.

Pam Brown, writer

A friend is the only person you will let into the house when you are Turning Out Drawers.

Pam Brown, writer

It's the friends you can call up at 4 a.m. that matter.

Marlene Dietrich, actor

Men kick friendship around like a football, but it doesn't seem to crack. Women treat it like glass and it goes to pieces.

Anne Morrow, writer and wife of Charles Lindbergh

You cannot prevent the birds of unhappiness from flying over your head, but you can prevent them from nesting in your hair.

Dillie Keane, comedian and singer-songwriter

The best time to make friends is before you need them.

Ethel Barrymore, actor

My two greatest needs and desires – smoking cigarettes and plotting revenge – are basically solitary pursuits.

Fran Lebowitz, writer and humorist

I have an antipathy towards shy people to this day, because I think it's lazy and dull.

Jenny Éclair, comedian

Being You!

The happy people are failures because they are on such good terms with themselves they don't give a damn.

Agatha Christie, crime writer

As soon as you forbid something, it thrives.

Rachel Stirling, actor

If you obey all the rules, you miss all the fun.

Katherine Hepburn, actor

The world wants to be cheated. So cheat.

Xaviera Hollander, writer and prostitute

The true place for commemoration is in your mind, not on your mantelpiece – and if your mind's too busy planning ahead, it isn't properly there at the time.

Victoria Coren, journalist

Our ability to delude ourselves may be an important survival tool.

Jane Wagner, writer and director

It is useless to hold a person to anything he says while he's in love, drunk or running for office.

Shirley MacLaine, actor and writer

Drugs have nothing to do with the creation of
music. In fact, drugs are dumb and self-indulgent.
Kind of like sucking your thumb.

Courtney Love, rock singer

Looks

I don't plan to grow old gracefully. I plan to have
face-lifts till my ears meet.

Rita Rudner, comedian

I am as fond of beauty spas as I am of being flayed
alive with barbed wire.

Kathy Lette, writer

I manage to look so young because I'm mentally
retarded.

Debbie Harry, rock singer

I always like to compare models to supermodels in
the way I compare Tampax to Super Tampax:
supermodels cost a bit more and they're a lot
thicker.

Jo Brand, comedian

Being You!

I just can't understand people who have ugly people working for them.

Jade Jagger, designer

I think that the longer I look good, the better gay men feel.

Cher, singer and actor

If I had been around when Rubens was painting, I would have been revered as a fabulous model. Kate Moss? Well, she would have been the paintbrush.

Dawn French, comedian

I've been trying to grow it, [her hair] but someone came up to me and asked if I was Enya. I was so shocked, I shaved all my hair off.

Sinead O'Connor, singer

After thirty, a body has a mind of its own.

Bette Midler, actor and singer

Even I don't wake up looking like Cindy Crawford.

Cindy Crawford, former model

Men are scared of me with short hair so I thought I'd grow it long to try to get a boyfriend.

Sonique, singer

Hair has always been important.

Diana Ross, singer

I won't wear skanky clothes that show off my booty, my belly or boobs. I have a great body. I could be Britney. I could be better than Britney.

Avril Lavigne, singer

I did not have implants, I just had a growth spurt.

Britney Spears, singer

It's an ill wind that blows when you leave the hairdresser.

Phyllis Diller, comedian

I have days when I just feel I look like a dog.

Michelle Pfeiffer, actor

My grandma was like, 'Oh Christina, you look like a whore!' I explained that's the idea.

Christina Aguilera, singer

I think it's really sad that a lot of women think that 'if I lose half a stone everything will be fine and everything will be perfect' but it won't – everything will be the same but you'll be a bit thinner.

Lorraine Kelly, TV presenter

Being You!

In Junior High a boy poured water down my shirt
and yelled: 'Now maybe they'll grow.'

Pamela Anderson, actor

My bottom is my delinquent daughter. I lavish
praise upon her cheeks when she's well-behaved
and when she gets out of control, I pretend she
isn't mine.

Anna Johnson, writer

You can have long hair, or you can have grey hair.
But you can't have both. So choose carefully.

Justin Rosenholtz, comedian

I am a big woman. I need big hair.

Aretha Franklin, singer

I knew I looked awful because my mother phoned
and said I looked lovely.

Comedian Jo Brand, after getting a makeover on TV

I have often depended on the blindness of strangers.

Adrienne E. Gusoff, teacher and writer

You have to be careful not to be upstaged by your
nipples.

Susan Sarandon, actor

Some months ago I went blonde, which is the only occasion in the whole of my political career when I have won one hundred per cent approval for something I have done.

Ann Widdecombe, British Member of Parliament

People always ask me how long it takes to do my hair. I don't know, I'm never there.

Dolly Parton, singer-songwriter

A woman could look like Godzilla, but if she's got blonde hair and a miniskirt, men start walking into walls.

Judy Tenuta, comedian

We have women in the military, but … they don't know if we can fight, if we can kill. I think we can. All the general has to do is walk over to the women and say, 'You see the enemy over there? They say you look fat in those uniforms.'

Elayne Boosler, comedian

A bit of lusting after someone does wonders for the skin.

Liz Hurley, actor

Being You!

What woman hasn't felt that her life's journey is part meat market, part catwalk?

Barbara Ellen, journalist

You could not have said that I was 'as cute as a speckled pup' without expecting the speckled pup to piss on your leg out of resentment.

Dolly Parton, singer-songwriter, on her childhood freckles

I'm not offended by all the dumb blonde jokes because I know I'm not dumb … and I also know that I'm not blonde.

Dolly Parton, singer-songwriter

I got out of Hastings when I was seventeen … stone.

Jo Brand, comedian

I have flabby thighs, but fortunately my stomach covers them.

Joan Rivers, comedian

Give me a dozen such heart-breaks, if that would help me to lose a couple of pounds.

Colette, novelist

No one loves a girl who needs to have her thighs taken in.

Barbara Ellen, journalist

Posh is just one operation behind me.

Glamour model Jordan on Victoria Beckham

If you're so worried that you have to cut your face up to make yourself happier, you're with the wrong guy.

Jerry Hall, model

Were my looks ever a burden? Gaad, no! I just wish I'd kissed more boys.

Debbie Harry, rock singer

If I hadn't been a woman, I'd have been a drag queen.

Dolly Parton, singer-songwriter

Wearing shorts is not a right, it's a privilege.

Justin Rosenholtz, comedian

It's amazing! All you have to do is look like crap on film and everyone thinks you're a brilliant actress.

Helen Mirren, actor

Being You!

If truth is beauty, how come no one has their hair done in the library?

Lily Tomlin, comedian

It's great being blonde – with such low expectations it's easy to impress.

Pamela Anderson, actor

If I showed you scripts from my first few movies, the descriptions of my characters all said 'the ugly girl'.

Winona Ryder, actor

I want to be a guy, but I want to wear a lot of make-up.

Gwen Stefani, rock singer

I often stop, flabbergasted, at the sight of this incredible thing that serves me as a face.

Simone de Beauvoir, writer

In Los Angeles everyone has perfect teeth. It's crocodile land.

Gwyneth Paltrow, actor

I'm going to have wrinkles really soon.

Cher, singer and actor

Looks

When we consider the significant cultural shifts of the past few years, the removal of Pamela Anderson's breast implants must rank right up there at the top.

Suzanne Moore, journalist

My memories of school have every girl in the class, except me, as blonde and pale as glasses of milk. This may explain my irrational, yet heartfelt hatred of Gwyneth Paltrow.

Emma Forrest, novelist

Every time I hear some smooth voice-over on a hair advertisement say, 'It's really important to have healthy, shiny hair', I think, not if you look like the back of a bus, it ain't.

Jo Brand, comedian

If the Nobel Prize was awarded by a woman, it would go to the inventor of the dimmer switch.

Kathy Lette, writer

It doesn't matter to me that you haven't seen your navel in twenty-five years and that you can wear your stomach as a kilt. Tell me you're happy.

Jennifer Saunders, comedian

Being You!

I was on a beach last summer, on a lovely beach sunbathing, and one of those lifeguards came up and he said to me, 'Madam you'll have to move – the tide wants to come in.'

Marjorie Rea, comedian

Patsy: Shahpari Khashoggi … All that money and she's still got a moustache … Look, darling, one more face-lift and she'd have a beard.

Comedian Jennifer Saunders as Edina in **Absolutely Fabulous**

When I appear in public people expect me to neigh, grind my teeth, paw the ground and swish my tail – none of which is easy.

Princess Anne

Outside every thin girl is a fat man trying to get in.

Katherine Whitehorn, journalist

I have eyes like a bullfrog, a neck like an ostrich and limp hair. You have to be good to survive with that equipment.

Bette Davis, actor

I'll do anything you want, but I won't dye my hair, change my wardrobe or lose weight.

Barbara Bush, former American First Lady

I'm not into working out. My philosophy: no pain, no pain.

Carol Leifer, writer and comedian

Any girl can be glamorous. All you have to do is stand still and look stupid.

Hedy Lamarr, actor

I don't have the time every day to put on make-up. I need that time to clean my rifle.

Henriette Mantel, actor

Clothes

I curse the day that I get a best-dressed award – then I'll be just ordinary.

Christina Aguilera, singer

I base most of my fashion taste on what doesn't itch.

Gilda Radner, comedian

I can make hemlines so short the world's your Gynaecologist.

Patsy from Absolutely Fabulous

Being You!

I can remember when pants were pants. You wore them for twenty years then you cut them down for pan scrubs. Or quilts.

Victoria Wood, comedian

I didn't even know my bra size until I made a movie.

Angelina Jolie, actor

Underwear is such an emotional thing.

Elle MacPherson, model

I don't judge others. I say if you feel good with what you're doing, let your freak flag fly.

Sarah Jessica Parker, actor

I always listen to *NSYNC's 'Tearin' Up My Heart'. It reminds me to wear a bra.

Britney Spears, singer

Sometimes you have to sacrifice your performance for high heels.

Gwen Stefani, rock singer

Never, ever buy clothes you intend to slim into or – oh, the possibility of it – gain weight to fill.

Karen Homer, style writer

Fashion is something that goes in one year and out the other.

Denise Klahn, writer

Friendship is not possible between two women, one of whom is very well-dressed.

Laurie Colwin, novelist

At the Billboard Awards my skirt was so tight they had to lift me on stage.

Beyonce Knowles, singer

Never trust a woman who doesn't have an instant hormonal response to diamonds.

Kate Reardon, fashion editor

I don't care for jewels. I love flowers. I like a fur coat here and there.

Ivana Trump, former model and ex-wife of Donald Trump

Some women hold up dresses that are so ugly and they always say the same thing: 'This looks much better on.' On what? On fire?

Rita Rudner, comedian

Being You!

Shoes inspire strong feelings in women.

Karen Homer, style writer

A woman's dress should be like a barbed-wire fence: serving its purpose without obstructing the view.

Sophia Loren, actor

I see girls in their miniskirts, their boobs hanging out and stuff. In Melbourne, the girls who wear that shit, they get beaten up. By other girls!

Holly Valance, actor and singer

Women dress alike all over the world: they dress to be annoying to other women.

Elsa Schiaparelli, designer

The upper-middle classes are never satisfied – they always take things back to shops and demand to have the sales assistant beaten.

Jenny Éclair, comedian

If high heels were so wonderful, men would be wearing them.

Sue Grafton, novelist

Anyone with more than three hundred and sixty-five pairs of shoes is a pig.

Barbara Melser Lieberman, writer

His shoes are slut pumps. You put on your Manolos and you find yourself saying 'Hi, Sailor' to every man that walks by.

Joan Rivers, comedian

Age

Youth is something very new: twenty years ago no one mentioned it.

Coco Chanel, designer

The lovely thing about being forty is that you can appreciate twenty-five-year-old men more.

Colleen McCullough, novelist

The hardest years in life are those between ten and seventy.

Helen Hayes, actor

Being You!

The secret of staying young is to live honestly, eat slowly, and lie about your age.

Lucille Ball, comedian and actor

I don't want to get to the end of my life and find that I have just lived the length of it. I want to have lived the width of it as well.

Diane Ackerman, poet and naturalist

There are only three ages for women in Hollywood – Babe, District Attorney, and Driving Miss Daisy.

Goldie Hawn, actor

All your age says about you is how long you've been alive.

Reverend Dianna Gwilliams, Anglican Vicar

As you get older, the pickings get slimmer, but the people don't.

Carrie Fisher, actor and writer

When I was sixteen all I wanted was to look like a forty-year-old divorcée.

Jenny Éclair, comedian

When I started, everyone said modelling only
lasted five years. Yeah, right.

Jerry Hall, model

I was a buffoon and an idiot until the age of forty.

Madonna, pop diva

I excessively hate to be forty. Not that I think it a
bad thing to be – only I'm not ready yet!

Edith Wharton, novelist

You don't need to retire as an actor, there are all
those parts you can play lying in bed, and in
wheelchairs.

Judi Dench, actor

Prior to *The Golden Girls*, when old people were
shown on television, you could almost smell them.

Bea Arthur, actor

Since I have also now reached the age when I
have positively not an eyelash of physical vanity
left: my clackers can rattle down to my flat feet
and my wig drop off in front of the howling mob
for all I care.

Caitlin Thomas, journalist

Being You!

I've never really been the right age for what I've been doing.

Elaine Dundy, writer

Please don't retouch my wrinkles. It took me so long to earn them.

Actor Anna Magnani to a photographer

I can remember saying helpfully to a new-made widow, aged about thirty-five: 'Never mind, you'll soon be dead, too.'

Gwen Raverat, artist

When I see a young girl I view her with the same pity that she views me with.

Lilli Palmer, actor

You want to look younger? Rent smaller children.

Phyllis Diller, comedian

If I get a grey hair and start to worry about it, I'll only get two more.

Grace Bumbry, opera singer

Age to women is like Kryptonite to Superman.

Kathy Lette, writer

It's the menopause. I've got my own climate.

Julie Walters, actor

I've outlived most of my body, and I'm trying so hard – oh, God, I've had so many things done to my body, when I die God won't know me.

Phyllis Diller, comedian

I've got enough crows' feet to start a bird sanctuary.

Kathy Lette, writer

Your mind is a cantankerous old computer that doesn't always remember how to access the old files.

Marge Piercy, writer

It is sad to grow old but nice to ripen.

Brigitte Bardot, actor and model

The problem with beauty is that it's like being born rich and getting poorer.

Joan Collins, actor

Old age is no place for sissies.

Bette Davis, actor

Being You!

The really frightening thing about middle age is the knowledge that you'll grow out of it.

Doris Day, actor and singer

So people think I'm lying about my age all the time? It's the records that are wrong. I've never told anyone how old I am. The minute they ask me I say 'That's none of your business.' So that means I've never once lied about my age. Now that's true!

Calista Flockhart, actor

Youth is a disease from which we all recover.

Dorothy Fulheim, writer

Like many women my age, I am 28 years old.

Mary Schmich, journalist

I cried on my 18th birthday. I thought 17 was such a nice age. You're young enough to get away with things, but you're old enough, too.

Liv Tyler, actor

You end up as you deserve. In old age you must put up with the face, the friends, the health, and the children you have earned.

Judith Viorst, poet

Remembering something at first try is now as good as an orgasm as far as I am concerned.

Gloria Steinem, writer

I blame Mother Nature (two-faced bitch!) and Father Time (bloody bastard!).

Kathy Lette, writer

You can judge your age by the amount of pain you feel when you come in contact with a new idea.

Pearl S. Buck, writer

Age is something that doesn't matter, unless you are a cheese.

Billie Burke, actor

If we wish to grow old gracefully we must commence by being young cheerfully.

Marie Corelli, novelist

My mother used to say: the older you get, the better you get – unless you're a banana.

Rose from The Golden Girls

My grandmother's ninety. She's dating. He's ninety-three. It's going great. They never argue. They can't hear each other.

Cathy Ladman, comedian

My grandmother started walking five miles a day when she was sixty. She's ninety-three today and we don't know where the hell she is.

Ellen DeGeneres, comedian

······ Confidence ······················

I've never had a humble opinion. If you've got an opinion, why be humble about it?

Joan Baez, singer-songwriter

Don't be humble. You're not that great.

Golda Meir, former Prime Minister of Israel

Most people who are as attractive, witty and intelligent as I am are usually conceited.

Joan Rivers, comedian

I'm an excellent talker. I've often said that I'd like to have my own talk show – with no guests.

Fran Lebowitz, writer and humorist

I don't try to be a sex bomb. I am one.

Kylie Minogue, pop diva

I'm not a diva. I'm a tadpole trying to be a frog.

Toni Braxton, pop singer

I don't worry about rivals. After all, there will never be another me.

Jordan, glamour model

I like exposing myself. There's not an awful lot that embarrasses me. I'm the kind of actress who absolutely believes in exposing herself.

Kate Winslet, actor

Sex appeal is 50 per cent what you've got and 50 per cent what people think you've got.

Sophia Loren, actor

I wasn't lucky. I deserved it.

Margaret Thatcher, former British Prime Minister

I am extraordinarily patient, provided I get my own way in the end.

Margaret Thatcher, former British Prime Minister

If I weren't as talented as I am ambitious, I would be a gross monstrosity.

Madonna, pop diva

I just have no more bad habits to give up.

Gwyneth Paltrow, actor

If I have a choice between the very horrible joke and the not so horrible, I'll always go for the very horrible one just because I enjoy that really. I like swearing as well.

Jo Brand, comedian

I am beautiful, famous and gorgeous. I could have any man in the world.

Anna Kournikova, tennis player and model

I think I've become more comfortable about being a human being.

Cameron Diaz, actor

I am just too much.

Bette Davis, actor

I rely on my personality for birth control.

Liz Winston, writer

Seize the moment. Remember all those women on the *Titanic* who waved off the dessert cart.

Erma Bombeck, writer and humorist

I only regret getting caught. I don't regret anything else.

Heidi Fleiss, madam

I don't suffer very much from guilt.

Joan Collins, actor

Life is about chasing after the things you truly think are worth it, even if they don't happen. I'd rather have nothing but know I didn't settle for something I didn't want.

Salma Hayek, actor

Stand up is ninety per cent front.

Jo Brand, comedian

The Problem
of 'Others'

Men

How many men does it take to tile a kitchen floor? Depends how thin you slice them.

Anonymous

There's something sexy about a gut. Not a 400-pound beer gut, but a little paunch. I love that.

Sandra Bullock, actor

I love a man who can wear my underwear

Yasmine Bleeth, actor

I love men, even though they're lying, cheating scumbags.

Gwyneth Paltrow, actor

The successful man is one who makes more than his wife can spend. And the successful woman is one who can find such a man.

Bienvenida Buck, formerly Lady Buck

The Problem of 'Others'

Women aren't funny. I know that because men are constantly telling me so.

Kathy Lette, writer

The most romantic piece of praise you can expect from an Australian man is 'Jeez luv, yer a grouse-looking Sheila.'

Sue Rhodes, novelist

I think men are sex objects – because they are only good for sex and not much else.

Jackie Weaver, actor

On the whole, barristers are more interested in their briefs than in a girl's.

Jilly Cooper, novelist

I only like two kinds of men: domestic and foreign.

Mae West, actor

I think men are very funny. If I had one of those dangly things stuffed down the front of my pants, I'd sit at home all day laughing at myself.

Dawn French, comedian

There is a moment when a man develops enough confidence and ease in a relationship to bore you to death.

Eve Babitz, novelist

I'd need a lobotomy to be equal to a man in Hollywood.

Roseanne, comedian

Men are very simple creatures. Emotionally they are blockheads.

Irma Kurtz, agony aunt

Men are emotional bonsai. You have to whack the fertiliser on to get any feelings out of them.

Kathy Lette, writer

The first time you buy a house you see how pretty the paint is and buy it. The second time you look to see if the basement has termites. It's the same with men.

Lupe Velez, actor

Giving a man space is like giving a dog a computer: the chances are he will not use it nicely.

Bette-Jane Raphael, writer

The Problem of 'Others'

Men don't know anything about pain; they've
never experienced labour, cramps or a bikini wax.

Nan Tisdale, writer

Anyone who believes that only time will tell has
never been in a boys' locker room.

Joan Rivers, comedian

No man has ever stuck his hand up your dress
looking for a library card.

Joan Rivers, comedian

Our mothers always told us that one day we would
meet our Mr Rights ... mind you, they told us not
to swim when we had our periods.

Kathy Lette, writer

Male heckler: 'Are you a lesbian?' – 'Are you my
alternative?'

Florence Kennedy, lawyer

Men only call themselves feminists in the hope of
getting a more intelligent fuck.

Kathy Lette, writer

If somebody makes me laugh, I'm his slave for life.

Bette Midler, actor

The only time a woman really succeeds in changing a man is when he's a baby.

Natalie Wood, actor

One of my theories is that men love with their eyes; women love with their ears.

Zsa Zsa Gabor, actor

Women speak because they wish to speak, whereas a man speaks only when driven to speech by something outside himself – like, for instance, he can't find any clean socks.

Jean Kerr, playwright

Once I went out with this guy who asked me to mother him – so I spat on a hanky and wiped his face.

Jenny Jones, comedian

A hard man's good to find – but you'll mostly find him asleep.

Mae West, actor

The Problem of 'Others'

Some of my best leading men have been horses and dogs.

Elizabeth Taylor, actor

How do I feel about men? With my fingers.

Cher, singer and actor

Women prefer men who have something tender about them – especially the legal kind.

Kay Ingram, writer

The fantasy of every Australian man is to have two women – one cleaning and the other dusting.

Maureen Murphy, actor

Man invented language to satisfy his need to complain.

Lily Tomlin, comedian

I never hated a man enough to give him back his diamonds.

Zsa Zsa Gabor, actor

A guy is a lump like a doughnut. So, first you gotta get rid of all the stuff his mum did to him, and then you gotta get rid of all that macho crap that they pick up from the beer commercials. And then there's my personal favourite, the male ego.

Roseanne, comedian

I believe in women. Men are just unsubstantiated rumours.

Erika Ritter, playwright

If men really knew how to do it, they wouldn't have to pay for it.

Roseanne, comedian

My ancestors wandered lost in the wilderness for forty years because even in biblical times, men would not stop to ask for directions.

Elayne Boosler, comedian

All that you suspect about women's friendships is true. We talk about dick size.

Cynthia Heimel, journalist

It is a truth universally acknowledged that one of the most significant problems of modern western society is the male of the species.

Melanie Phillips, journalist

The Problem of 'Others'

Listen, if it's got four wheels or a dick you're goin'a have trouble with it guaranteed.

Annie Proulx, novelist

There are so many kinds of awful men – one can't avoid them all.

Wendy Cope, poet

Men are luxuries, not necessities.

Cher, singer and actor

Maleness remains a recessive genetic trait like colour-blindness and haemophilia.

Elizabeth Gould Davis, writer and pregnancy specialist

Why are we supposed to be with men, anyway? I feel like I used to know.

Lorrie Moore, novelist

Doesn't it feel like you live on the Planet of Guys?

Kate Clinton, comedian

My mother's two categories; nice men did things for you, bad men did things to you.

Margaret Atwood, novelist

There's nineteen men living in my neighbourhood.
Eighteen of them are fools and the other one ain't
no doggone good.

Bessie Smith, blues singer

His mother should have thrown him away and kept
the stork.

Mae West, actor

To rephrase Samuel Butler, a man is simply a
woman's way of making another woman.

Naomi Segal, feminist writer

When God created man, she was only joking.

Graffiti

I don't know how men are different from hogs …
They chase after the same things: food, drink,
women.

Emilia Pardo Bazan, writer and critic

Most single men don't even like people. They live
like bears with furniture.

Rita Rudner, comedian

The Problem of 'Others'

I'd like to get to the point where I can be just as mediocre as a man.

Juanita Kreps, economist

Men think they're more important than women because their suit jackets have secret pockets on the inside.

Rita Rudner, comedian

All men are children, and if you understand that, a woman understands everything.

Coco Chanel, designer

Until Eve gave him the apple, [Adam] didn't even know he was wearing underpants.

Paula Yates, TV presenter

This is the man who, as far as inventions go, thinks Wonderbra and La Perla are up there with the wheel.

Jane Moore, writer

Under thirty-five a man has too much to learn, and I don't have time to teach him.

Hedy Lamarr, actor

Men are not stupid, or at least not too stupid to realise that if they didn't get sensitive real fast, they weren't going to get laid any more.

Cynthia Heimel, journalist

All men are unreasonable; it is their normal state.

Anne Mathews, writer

I am tired of being a free finishing school for men.

Suzanne Wolstenholme, writer

And their hobbies! … Why? Why? Only a man could think that getting a miniature plane off the ground was time well spent.

Lucy Ellmann, novelist

You can talk to a man about any subject. He won't understand, but you can talk to him.

Anonymous

Because he has such respect for your superior wisdom and technical know-how, he is constantly asking questions like 'Does this kid need a sweater?' or 'Is the baby wet?'

Jean Kerr, playwright

The Problem of 'Others'

Only a divinity could determine which is funnier,
Man's Dream of Woman, or Woman as she is.

Miriam Beard, writer

Men have to learn things that women have known
for centuries.

Toni Halliday, singer

Perhaps the predilection of men for rapine and
slaughter should be interpreted as meaning that
men are premenstrual at all times.

Germaine Greer, feminist writer and academic

Nuclear bombs, fluorescent lights, burning witches
at the stake, deciding animals have no emotions –
only men could have come up with such ideas.

Lucy Ellmann, novelist

Men are so ethical, they let us die for their
principles!

Lucy Ellmann, novelist

There are a lot of women who live with pot-bellied
pigs.

Catherine Zeta-Jones, actor

Men are beasts and even beasts don't behave as they do.

Brigitte Bardot, actor

Beneath the thick skin of the stronger sex lies an open wound called the Male Ego.

Letty Cottin Pogrebin, novelist

If men liked shopping, they'd call it research.

Cynthia Nelms, writer

I moved to Los Angeles when I was twenty-one. I felt like a kid in a candy shop. I'd be driving down the road and – Mmmm! There was a guy and Mmmm! There was a guy!

Tori Amos, singer

Nine out of ten males will believe anything, especially if it confirms their virility.

Andrea Martin, comedian

Beware of men who cry. It's true that men who cry are sensitive and in touch with feelings, but the only feelings they tend to be sensitive and in touch with are their own.

Nora Ephron, writer and humorist

The Problem of 'Others'

They say men enjoy shaving – it's the one time each day they get to look in the mirror and say, 'Hey there, you handsome devil!'

Helen Gurley Brown, journalist

Research has shown that men usually sleep on the right side of the bed. Even in their sleep they have to be right.

Rita Rudner, comedian

What say we reduce men to their normal size so that they'll fit into our life?

Cynthia Heimel, journalist

I think women have a different spirituality to men. We share the same emotions basically, but social structures always have been set up by men ... Even Tampax is made by men.

K.D. Lang, singer-songwriter

Whatever women do they must do twice as well as men to be thought half as good. Luckily this is not difficult.

Charlotte Whitton, former Mayor of Ottawa

Men are judged as the sum of their parts while women are judged as some of their parts.

Julie Burchill, journalist

Don't accept rides from strange men, and remember that all men are strange as hell.

Robin Morgan, poet and journalist

One hopes they have to leave early in the morning to go to school.

Writer Fran Lebowitz, on lovers who stay overnight

Men are brave enough to go to war, but they are not brave enough to get a bikini wax.

Rita Rudner, comedian

The main difference between men and women is that men are lunatics and women are idiots.

Rebecca West, novelist

As far as I'm concerned, being any gender is a drag.

Patti Smith, rock singer

Talking with a man is like trying to saddle a cow. You work like hell, but what's the point?

Gladys Upham, writer

The Problem of 'Others'

What every woman knows and no man can ever grasp is that even if he brings home everything on the list, he will still not have got the right things.

Allison Pearson, journalist

Don't say anything important if the sports section is within 10 feet.

Kristin van Ogtrop, journalist

Why did God create men? Because vibrators can't mow the lawn.

Anonymous

The male has the negative Midas touch – everything he touches turns to shit.

Valerie Solanas, feminist writer

Unlike women, men menstruate by shedding other people's blood.

Lucy Ellmann, novelist

When women are depressed, they eat or go shopping. Men invade another country. It's a whole different way of thinking.

Elayne Boosler, comedian

God gave women intuition and femininity. Used properly, the combination easily jumbles the brain of any man I've ever met.

Farrah Fawcett, actor

Don't look at him as a Republican but as the man I love. And if that doesn't work, look at him as someone who can squash you.

Maria Shriver Kennedy, introducing Arnold Schwarzenegger to her family

When I eventually met Mr Right I had no idea that his first name was Always.

Rita Rudner, comedian

···· Other Women ················

Lesbianism has always seemed to me an extremely inventive response to the shortage of men but otherwise not worth the trouble.

Nora Ephron, writer and humorist

So why exactly do they call you Posh?

Model Naomi Campbell to Victoria Beckham

The Problem of 'Others'

Only good girls keep diaries. Bad girls don't have
time.

Tallulah Bankhead, actor

She saw a sign saying 'Wet Floor.' So she did!

Joan Rivers, comedian

As far as I'm concerned, Emma Bunton wouldn't
have got through the auditions on 'Popstars'.

Kym Marsh, pop singer

We don't have a problem. I don't think about her. I
don't care about her, because I don't deal with the
devil.

Lil Kim on fellow rapper Foxy Brown

I think she's unpleasant, a right snob. It would be
unoriginal for her to have a go at me now.

'It' girl Tara Palmer-Tomkinson on Lady Victoria Hervey

A lucky model who's been given a lot of
opportunities I just wish she would have done
more with.

Actor and singer Jennifer Lopez on Cameron Diaz

I'm eight years younger, 3 inches taller and I've got boobs!

Actor Sophie Marceau on Isabelle Adjani

A woman went to a plastic surgeon and asked him to make her like Bo Derek. He gave her a lobotomy.

Joan Rivers, comedian

She's got a great-looking husband, a little boy and all the money in the world. She hasn't got the looks, but you can't have everything.

Glamour model Jordan on Victoria Beckham

The only way you can prevent people from talking about you when you leave the room is to never leave the room ... Don't go to lunch. Don't go to the bathroom – wear a catheter if necessary.

Ellen DeGeneres, comedian

An anorexic transvestite.

TV presenter Carol Vorderman on TV style guru Trinny Woodall

A carthorse in a badly fitting bin liner.

TV presenter Carol Vorderman on TV style guru Susannah Constantine

The Problem of 'Others'

She looks like she combs her hair with an egg beater.

Gossip columnist Louella Parsons on Joan Collins

As an actress her only flair is her nostrils.

Film critic Pauline Kael on Candice Bergen

She has two expressions – joy and indigestion.

Writer and wit Dorothy Parker on Marion Davies

The emotional, sexual, and psychological stereotyping of females begins when the doctor says: It's a girl.

Shirley Chisholm, congresswoman

Elizabeth Taylor has more chins than a Chinese telephone directory.

Joan Rivers, comedian

What's the use of having a totally gorgeous body like Victoria Principle if you've got a mind like ... Victoria Principle?

Jean Kittson, actor and writer

Quite frankly I've never understood what Jagger saw in that buck-toothed nag in the first place.

Academic Camille Paglia on Jerry Hall

Camilla could have done so much better.

Journalist India Knight on Prince Charles

Some women are better than others at being female.

Jenny Éclair, comedian

My girlfriends are usually making 'Who lit the fuse on your tampon?' taunts by now.

Kathy Lette, writer

I refuse to be a female impersonator. I am a woman.

Germaine Greer, feminist writer and academic

Women used to have time to make mince pies and had to fake orgasms. Now we can manage the orgasms, but we have to fake the mince pies. And they call this progress.

Allison Pearson, journalist

Women never have young minds. They are born three thousand years old.

Shelagh Delaney, playwright

Posterity is full of men who seized the day, while the women were planning for a fortnight on Tuesday.

Allison Pearson, journalist

The Problem of 'Others'

Voting for [Margaret Thatcher, former British Prime Minister] was like buying a Vera Lynn LP, getting it home and finding 'Never Mind the Bollocks' inside the red, white and blue sleeve.

Julie Burchill, journalist

Men like cars, women like clothes. Women only like cars because they take them to the clothes.

Rita Rudner, comedian

It is extremely tacky for a friend to mention a friend's weight to her face. Behind her back is a different thing altogether.

Cynthia Heimel, writer

Behind almost every woman you ever heard of stands a man who let her down.

Naomi Bliven, novelist

If there is anything more boring to me than the problems of big-busted women, it is the problems of beautiful women.

Nora Ephron, writer and humorist

She'd never make the same mistake again: she always made a new mistake instead.

Wendy Cope, poet

Brains are a handicap for a blonde.

Paula Yates, TV presenter

Such an attractive lass. So outdoorsy. She loves nature in spite of what it did to her.

Actor and singer Bette Midler on Princess Anne

In my day, women were still stud beasts, and feminine wit wasn't fashionable. It was a privilege reserved exclusively to the men.

Rachel Ferguson, novelist

The great and almost only comfort about being a woman is that one can always pretend to be more stupid than one is, and no one is surprised.

Freya Stark, writer

I went to a girls' school and it made me so stupid that I could barely remember how to breathe.

India Knight, journalist

She thinks Bosnia Herzegovina's the Wonderbra model.

Isabel Wolff, journalist

The Problem of 'Others'

And yes, making Posh Spice look dumb didn't turn out to be all that hard.

Zoe Williams, journalist

There is actually no age limit to being a slag, it just gets sadder as you get older.

Jenny Éclair, comedian

When the chips are down, every woman must realise she is sitting on her fortune.

Germaine Greer, feminist writer and academic

Smart girls know how to play tennis, piano and dumb.

Lynne Redgrave, actor

Women are one of the Almighty's enigmas to prove to men that he knows more than they do.

Ellen Glasgow, novelist

Whatever they try and sell you, the best aphrodisiac for women is eating oysters because if you can swallow oysters, you can swallow anything.

Hattie Hayridge, comedian

Being a woman is of special interest only to aspiring male transsexuals. To actual women it is simply a good excuse not to play football.

Fran Lebowitz, writer and humorist

I'm the intelligent, independent-type woman. In other words, a girl who can't get a man.

Shelley Winters, actor

It's time to stop denying the 'inner bitch' in ourselves. Stop apologising for her. Set her free.

Elizabeth Hilts, journalist

When a man gives his opinion he's a man. When a woman gives her opinion she's a bitch.

Bette Davis, actor

Men have power and a power complex; women just have a complex.

Yvonne Roberts, feminist writer

The most indolent women have been seen running to catch a boss.

Jilly Cooper, novelist

The Problem of 'Others'

Always be nice to other girls. If you don't, they will find some underhand way of getting even with you.

Elizabeth Hawes, fashion writer

Girls have got balls. They're just a little higher up, that's all.

Joan Jett, rock singer

Were women *meant* to do everything – work and have babies?

Candice Bergen, actor

People call me a feminist whenever I express sentiments that differentiate me from a doormat or a prostitute.

Rebecca West, novelist

A woman scorned is a woman who quickly learns her way around a courtroom.

Colette Mann

You can lead a whore to culture but you can't make her think.

Dorothy Parker, writer and wit

Women's virtue is man's greatest invention.

Cornelia Otis Skinner, actor

There are two categories of women – those who are women and those who are men's wives.

Charlotte Whitton, former Mayor of Ottawa

Why is it that *The Oxford Dictionary of Quotations* bulges with quotations by men ... when women (as men are the first to point out) do all the talking?

Peg Bracken, food writer

Many militant women show too plainly by their inefficiency, their obesity and their belligerence, that they have not succeeded in finding any measure of liberation in their own company.

Germaine Greer, feminist writer and academic

The only difference between men and women is that women are able to create new little human beings in their bodies while ... doing everything men do.

Erica Jong, novelist

He accused me of the thing men think is the most insulting thing they can accuse you of – wanting to be married.

Nora Ephron, writer and humorist

The Problem of 'Others'

In her world, men loved women as the fox loves the hare. And women loved men as the tapeworm loves the gut.

Pat Barker, novelist

I've no time for broads who want to rule the world alone. Without men, who'd do up the zipper on the back of your dress?

Bette Davis, actor

Poor Mary Ann! She gave the guy an inch and now he thinks he's a ruler.

Mae West, actor

The vote, I thought, means nothing to women. We should be armed.

Edna O'Brien, novelist

 **Family**

My grandmother was a very tough woman. She buried three husbands. Two of them were just napping.

Rita Rudner, comedian

Family

Some of my colleagues are so keen on family values that they choose to have more than one of them.

Edwina Currie, former Member of Parliament

Family are the main source of guilt and therefore must be got rid of, either by suffocation or alienation.

Jenny Éclair, comedian

Two women a week are currently being murdered by the man they live with and one child a week by its father or stepfather – but hey, the family that slays together stays together!

Julie Burchill, journalist

My parents and I are very close … genetically.

Wendy Liebman, comedian

You hear a lot of dialogue on the death of the American family. Families aren't dying. They're merging into big conglomerates.

Erma Bombeck, writer and humorist

Me? An angel! just ask my mum about that!

Charlotte Church, singer

The Problem of 'Others'

Mum comes in and says 'I'm working out,' and
she'll just be standing there naked doing a dance.

Kelly Osbourne, pop singer

All I heard when I was growing up was 'Why can't
you be more like your cousin Sheila? Why can't you
be more like your cousin Sheila?' Sheila died at birth.

Joan Rivers, comedian

There's some sort of mother blood that just wants
you to buy firearms when you have a child.

Courtney Love, rock singer

I think it's a mother's duty to embarrass their
children.

Cher, singer and actor

I've always blamed my shortcomings as a mother
on the fact that I studied Child Psychology and
Discipline under an unmarried professor whose
only experience was in raising a dog.

Erma Bombeck, writer and humorist

Give a child what it wants and it's gone forever.

Fay Weldon, writer

In Australia, breeding is something we do with dogs.

Kathy Lette, writer

Even though all fathers are physically exhausted and mentally denuded, they like to talk. Encourage Dad to talk. Probably no one has for years.

Elizabeth Hawes, fashion designer

If Everybody Else's Mother turned up at a PTA meeting and identified herself, she would be lynched.

Erma Bombeck, writer and humorist

Grannies are only cute on TV. In real life they're like Oxfam shops on legs.

Pamela Stephenson, actor and writer

Of course, I could always depend on my brothers to tell me how bad I looked.

Dolly Parton, singer-songwriter

Family to me is closely associated, with, like, strapping 500-pound bricks to my feet and jumping in the water.

Drew Barrymore, actor

Sometimes I think that the roles of housewife and practising Christian are quite incompatible.

Rosamund Dashwood, novelist

21st Century Living

Work

Some people spend their lives failing and never notice.

Judith Rossner, writer

If lawyers are disbarred and clergymen defrocked, doesn't it follow that electricians can be delighted; musicians denoted; cowboys deranged; models deposed; tree surgeons debarked, and dry cleaners depressed.

Victoria Ostman, writer

There is no pleasure in having nothing to do; the fun is in having lots to do and not doing it.

Mary Little

First things first, second things never.

Shirley Conran, writer

21st Century Living

I've always wanted to be a spy, and frankly I'm a little surprised that British intelligence has never approached me.

Liz Hurley, actor

I'm a bitter ender.

Tallulah Bankhead, actor

Always suspect any job men willingly vacate for a woman.

Jill Tweedie, journalist

When people said to me, 'Do you feel that you opened the door for these other women?' I had assumed that they were open and I was just walking through like everyone else.

Suzanne Vega, singer-songwriter

The women's movement has made a huge difference ... There are women doctors and women lawyers. There are anchorwomen, although most of them are blonde.

Nora Ephron, writer

Toughness doesn't have to come in a pinstripe suit.

Dianne Feinstein, former Mayor of San Francisco

People are terrified when I ask them to come with me into a small room.

Martha Lane Fox, co-owner of Lastminute.com

Don't cook. Don't clean. No man will ever make love to a woman because she waxed the linoleum – 'My God, the floor's immaculate. Lie down, you hot bitch.'

Joan Rivers, comedian

I hate housework! You make the beds, you do the dishes – and six months later you have to start all over again.

Joan Rivers, comedian

When men do dishes it's called helping. When women do dishes it's called life.

Anna Quinlin, novelist

Housework can kill you if done right.

Erma Bombeck, writer

When Sears comes out with a riding vacuum cleaner, then I'll clean the house.

Roseanne, comedian

A dish that don't survive the dishwasher don't deserve to live.

Liz Scott, actor

Nature abhors a vacuum and so do I.

Anne Gibbons, cartoonist

In politics, if you want anything said, ask a man; if you want anything done, ask a woman.

Margaret Thatcher, former British Prime Minister

Housework can't kill you, but why take a chance?

Phyllis Diller, comedian

Domestic Goddesses who say they get high on housework have obviously been inhaling too much cleaning fluid.

Kathy Lette, writer

It's a small world ... but not if you have to clean it.

Anonymous

Scrubbing ... doesn't seem to me to be a human occupation at all. I'd rather keep the floor moist and grow a crop of grass on it.

Katherine Mansfield, writer

I buried a lot of my ironing in the back yard.

Phyllis Diller, comedian

A woman fit to be a man's wife is too good to be his servant.

Dorothy L. Sayers, novelist

The starring role of Housewife – a woman who married a house.

Maeve Binchy, novelist

 # Success

The trouble with the rat race is that, even if you win, you're still a rat.

Lily Tomlin, comedian

When in doubt, do what someone successful does.

Suze Orman, writer

Too often, the opportunity knocks, but by the time you push back the chain, push back the bolt, unhook the two locks and shut off the burglar alarm, it's too late.

Rita Coolidge, singer

21st Century Living

The worst part of having success is to try finding someone who is happy for you.

Bette Midler, actor and singer

Mrs Clinton's shown the way to power is paved with matrimony.

Helen Stevenson, writer

Don't confuse fame with success. Madonna is one; Helen Keller is the other.

Erma Bombeck, writer and humorist

I always wanted to be somebody, but now I realise I should have been more specific.

Lily Tomlin, comedian

I mean what's so fulfilling about fulfilment anyway?

Maureen Lipman, actor

I am rich and famous. I have a talented and gorgeous husband and two beautiful children. I could go on.

Madonna, pop diva

Behind every successful man is a woman with a brush and shovel cleaning up the shit he's too full of himself to notice.

Raquel Welch, actor

Happiness is good health and a bad memory.

Ingrid Bergman, actor

You can only sleep your way to the middle.

Dawn Steel, film executive

The more flesh you show, the further up the ladder you go.

Kim Basinger, actor

I can't tell you how many times I've been asked by people 'Do you think race and gender contributed to your success?' How the heck do I know? I can't repackage myself as a white male and see whether I would have gotten this far.

Condoleezza Rice, US Presidential advisor

The more things you have, the more people you need to employ to look after them.

Billie Piper, singer and actor

If I had my life to live again, I'd make the same mistakes, only sooner.

Tallulah Bankhead, actor

Show me a person who has never made a mistake and I'll show you somebody who has never achieved much.

Joan Collins, actor

It was George Hamilton who said the immortal line, 'Joan, better to be a shrewd business woman than a screwed actress.'

Joan Collins, actor

It's not whether you win or lose – it's how you lay the blame.

Fran Lebowitz, writer and humorist

I may not be making a living, but I'm making a difference.

Rachel Hickerson, feminist

····· **Technology** ·····················

For a list of all the ways technology has failed to improve the quality of life, please press three.

Alice Kahn, scientist and writer

What should you give a man who has everything?
A woman to show him how to work it.

Anonymous

The C-drive on my (faulty) computer tells me every
morning that it has spent the night de-
fragmenting, and I feel sympathy with it.

Fay Weldon, writer

It is the modern equivalent of nasty little boys
ringing doorbells and running away.

Journalist Libby Purves on computer viruses

The telephone is a good way to talk to people
without having to offer them a drink.

Fran Lebowitz, writer and humorist

Millions long for immortality who do not know
what to do with themselves on a rainy Sunday
afternoon.

Susan Ertz, writer

Since mobile phones, lying has become much
easier, much more routine.

Barbara Ellen, journalist

Excuse me, everybody, I have to go to the bathroom. I really have to telephone, but I'm too embarrassed to say so.

Dorothy Parker, writer and wit

To attract men, I wear a perfume called 'New Car Interior'.

Rita Rudner, comedian

We're so busy flicking channels these days that we miss the best programmes. The same can certainly be said for our relationships.

Mariella Frostrup, TV presenter

Television has proved that people will look at anything rather than each other.

Ann Landers, journalist

We love television because television brings us a world in which television does not exist.

Barbara Ehrenreich, writer

There are days when any electrical appliance in the house, including the vacuum cleaner, offers more entertainment than the TV set.

Harriet Van Horne, writer

Money

It wasn't until I met my boyfriend Grant that I realised it is actually illegal for large-breasted women to handle money.

Gayle Tuesday, Page Three Stunner, aka Brenda Gilhooley

I get so tired of listening to one million dollars here, one million dollars there. It's so petty.

Imelda Marcos, former First Lady of the Philippines

If you want to know what God thinks of money, just look at the people he gave it to.

Dorothy Parker, writer and wit

I don't have a bank account because I don't know my mother's maiden name.

Paula Poundstone, comedian

He was so mean it hurt him to go to the bathroom.

Actor Britt Ekland on Rod Stewart

Let me tell you something, Mister. If I had her money, I'd be richer than she is.

Audrey Hepburn in Breakfast at Tiffany's

21st Century Living

Whoever said money can't buy happiness simply didn't know where to go shopping.

Bo Derek, actor and model

Look at the amounts Ben Affleck has lavished on J-Lo. When Nic opens his wallet, moths fly out.

Lisa Marie Presley on Nicolas Cage

I have an expensive hobby: buying homes, redoing them, tearing them down and building them up the way they want to be built. I want to be an architect.

Sandra Bullock, actor

In spite of the cost of living, it's still popular.

Kathy Norris

If you want to say it with flowers, a single rose says: 'I'm cheap!'

Delta Burke, actor

Some people think they are worth a lot of money just because they have it.

Fannie Hurst, writer

The two most beautiful words in the English language are 'cheque enclosed'.

Dorothy Parker, writer and wit

Girls just want to have funds.

Adrienne E. Gusoff, writer and teacher

Some people get so rich they lose all respect for humanity. That's how rich I want to be.

Rita Rudner, comedian

If I didn't have some kind of education, then I wouldn't be able to count my money.

Missy Elliot, singer

Where large sums of money are concerned, it is advisable to trust nobody.

Agatha Christie, crime writer

Nothing buys happiness, but money can certainly hire it for short periods.

Irma Kurtz, agony aunt

I won't get out of bed for less than $10,000 a day.

Linda Evangelista, former model

Anyone seeing women at a bargain-basement sale … sees aggression that would make Attila the Hun turn pale.

Estelle Ramey, physician and physiologist

Look, I grew up in a goddamn shack, so I like a bit of comfort.

Mariah Carey, singer

I was born ostentatious. They will list my name in the dictionary some day. They will use 'Imeldific' to mean ostentatious extravagance.

Imelda Marcos, former First Lady of the Philippines

I don't know where the money went – it just went. I don't even like shopping

Sarah Ferguson, former Duchess of York

It's amazing how healing money can be.

Dolly Parton, singer-songwriter and actor

It wasn't until I got divorced that I understood the value of money.

Melanie B, singer

As times get harder, words grow more weaselly. Euphemisms boom in a recession, even if nothing else does.

Alison Eadie, journalist

Never economise on luxuries.

Angela Thirkell, novelist

The most popular labour saving device is still money.

Phyllis George, actor and broadcaster

I'm overdrawn at the bank. I won't say how much, but if you saw it written down, you'd think it was a sex chatline number.

Julie Burchill, journalist

I've been poor and I've been rich. Rich is better.

Fanny Brice, comedian

Our phone bill is equivalent to the national debt of Vanuatu.

Isabel Wolff, journalist

Yuppies, we knew, were greedy, shallow and small … We renamed the seven dwarves: Artsy, Fartsy, Cranky, Sleazy, Beasty, Dud and Yuppie.

Lorrie Moore, novelist

He who buys what he does not want, will soon want what he cannot buy.

Anne Mathews, writer

I always say it doesn't pay to economise. It's the extravagant women who are most respected by their husbands.

Fannie Hurst, writer

······· Celebrity ·······

I think Mick Jagger would be astounded and amazed if he realised how to many people he is not a sex symbol.

Angie Bowie, former wife of David Bowie

I have to be seen to be believed.

Queen Elizabeth II

I don't care what is written about me so long as it isn't true.

Dorothy Parker, writer and wit

I was very shaky on stage. I made a million-pound bet with my agent five minutes before that I wouldn't win so I was very shocked. I was very shaken – if you lose a million pounds five minutes before, it is very shaky.

Actor Judi Dench on the 2002 Baftas

Madam Tussaud's are very angry. Not only have I got new hairstyles, I've also got new tattoos.

Melanie C, singer

I welcome him like I welcome cold sores. He's from England, he's angry and he's got Mad Power Disease.

Singer Paula Abdul on Simon Cowell

You can't get spoiled if you do your own ironing.

Meryl Streep, actor

I'd like Jennifer Lopez to play me in a film of my life.

Kacey Ainsworth, actor

Better than cystitis.

Comedian Jo Brand's suggested slogan to boost
John Major's popularity

The censors wouldn't even let me sit on a guy's lap, and I've been on more laps than a table napkin.

Mae West, actor

My performances tend to be a little bit off-centre, whatever that means.

Rachel Weisz, actor

I don't use the voice of Bart when I'm making love to my husband, but Marge's voice turns him on a little.

Actor Nancy Cartwright, voice of Bart Simpson

Sting! I mean, come on – who doesn't love Sting? Even if you love Megadeath, you have respect for Sting. If you love Pokemon, you'll find out who Sting is someday.

Jenna Elfman, actor

The movie business divides women into ice queens and sluts, and there have been times I wanted to be a slut more than anything.

Sigourney Weaver, actor

I could get into bed with James Bond, then take my false leg off and it would really be a gun.

Heather Mills, former model

I said, 'You have got to be kidding. I am an ape and yet I am still expected to squeeze myself into one of those damn things.'

Helena Bonham Carter, actor

A movie camera is like having someone you have a crush on watching you from afar – you pretend it's not there.

Darryl Hannah, actor

In school nativity plays I was always the bloody little donkey, I was never Mary.

Geri Halliwell, pop singer

The best thing I have is the knife from *Fatal Attraction*. I hung it in my kitchen. It's my way of saying, Don't mess with me.

Glenn Close, actor

Today, watching television often means fighting, violence and foul language – and that's just deciding who gets to hold the remote control.

Donna Gephart, journalist

You know you've made it when you've been moulded in miniature plastic. But you know what children do with Barbie dolls – it's a bit scary, actually.

Carrie Fisher, actor

21st Century Living

I saw Emma Bunton and insisted on talking to her. I tapped her on the shoulder and stood there like a lemon. I wanted to tell her how brilliant she was. Instead I said something like, 'Great woman!' It wasn't my finest moment.

Daisy Donovan, TV presenter

I certainly hope I'm not still answering child-star questions by the time I reach menopause.

Christina Ricci, actor

I don't mean to be a diva, but some days you wake up and you're Barbra Streisand.

Courtney Love, rock singer

Can you see me being like Steps? I don't think so. My music is much more mature and more meaningful.

Caprice, model

At the studio she said hello to everyone but me. She thought I was there just to make the drinks.

Christina Millian on Jennifer Lopez for whom she wrote the hit song 'Play'

If I pop everyone who calls me a diva then I'm going to spend the rest of my life in prison.

Chaka Khan, singer

Mum, have I sung at the Hollywood Bowl?

Charlotte Church, singer

On staying the night at Elton John's: It was adorable. He had all these porcelain kitty-cats everywhere. We woke up and had breakfast together in robes and everything. It was so cute.

Anastacia, singer

Hollywood's a place where they'll pay you a thousand dollars for a kiss, and fifty cents for your soul. I know, because I turned down the first offer often enough and held out for the fifty cents.

Marilyn Monroe, actor

How did you all meet?

TV presenter Donna Air interviewing sibling group the Corrs

There's no drugs, no Tom in a dress, no psychiatrists.

Nicole Kidman, actor

When someone follows you all the way to the shop and watches you buy toilet roll, you know your life has changed.

Jennifer Aniston, actor

I wanted to be a nun. I saw nuns as superstars …
When I was growing up I went to a Catholic school,
and the nuns, to me, were these superhuman,
beautiful, fantastic people.

Madonna, pop diva

I think that [the film] *Clueless* was very deep. I
think it was deep in the way that it was very light. I
think lightness has to come from a very deep place
if it's true lightness.

Alicia Silverstone, actor

I've never been so excited to have people walk all
over me for the rest of my life.

Actor Nicole Kidman on receiving her Walk of Fame star

It's so bad being homeless in winter. They should
buy a plane ticket and go somewhere hot like the
Caribbean where they can eat free fish all day.

Lady Victoria Hervey, 'It' girl

Every time an Oscar is given out, an agent gets his
wings.

Kathy Bates, actor

I have to be careful to get out before I become the grotesque caricature of a hatchet-faced woman with big knockers.

Jamie Lee Curtis, actor

You've no idea how many men I've had to sleep with to win this.

Kim Catrall, actor

Everyone wants to ride with you in the limo, but what you need is someone who will take the bus with you when the limo breaks down.

Oprah Winfrey, TV presenter

I don't get Robbie Williams. I think he seems rude and he's always getting his knickers off.

Gwyneth Paltrow, actor

I have to remind my dad, 'Journalists – no matter how many cigars they smoke with you – are not your friends, so don't talk to them.'

Cameron Diaz, actor

We were so terrific together. Her so tall with all that hair. Me so tall with no hair.

Former model Grace Jones on her party days with Jerry Hall

I behaved badly only because I felt superior to all who surrounded me.

Sarah Bernhardt, comedian

It's a shame to call somebody a 'diva' simply because they work harder than everybody else.

Jennifer Lopez, singer and actor

Egotism – usually just a case of mistaken nonentity.

Barbara Stanwyck, actor

Success has killed more than bullets.

Texas Guinan, night-club queen

I get completely slagged off by people whose mortgage I'm paying. They write 500 words about me, they pay their mortgage that week.

Tracy Emin, artist

Do ya think Rod's sexy? I'm not even sure he's still alive.

Barbara Ellen, journalist

Jackie Onassis was one smart woman, believe me. She knew. God gave women sex so we can shop the next day.

Joan Rivers, comedian

At the Gap they have a special changing cubicle just for celebrities – it's just like all the others except it has a star on the door and a bowl of fruit inside.

Ellen DeGeneres, comedian

I don't see myself certainly as a celebrity, as a star, because people are so familiar with me ... Basically, people say 'Hey Oprah, come on over here and sit down.' Every day, at the end of the show, they say, 'Want to go to lunch, want to come to my house? I'm fixing so and so for dinner.'

Oprah Winfrey, TV presenter

I want to be more famous than anyone, ever. If it means I can't go to the shops without being mobbed, I won't mind.

Patsy Kensit, actor

I just want them to catch me with my dad and try to turn it into some 'handsome, mystery hunk'.

Singer Andrea Corr on the paparazzi

One of my first boyfriends said in an interview, 'If Jennifer wasn't on TV right now, she'd be in Mexico singing in front of five people in a restaurant.'

Jennifer Lopez, singer and actor

I realised I should try harder to be an actress
because I'd never make it as a waitress.

Jane Krakowski, actor

In rock, you are nothing until you've slept with
Winona Ryder and had a feud with me.

Courtney Love, rock singer

God, I can be difficult when I want to be.

Judi Dench, actor

The trouble with being a princess is that it is so
hard to have a pee.

Diana, Princess of Wales

I stopped believing in Santa Claus when I was six.
Mother took me to see him in a department store,
and he asked for my autograph.

Shirley Temple, actor

I used to be snow-white until I drifted.

Mae West, actor

I always tell film-makers I'm happy to run around
in the buff if the co-star runs around with his willy
hanging out.

Michelle Pfeiffer, actor

I've made so many movies playing a hooker that they don't pay in the regular way any more. They leave it on the dresser.

Shirley MacLaine, actor and writer

The only 'ism' Hollywood believes in is plagiarism.

Dorothy Parker, writer and wit

Actresses will happen in the best regulated families.

Ethel Watts Munford, writer

It was a dull week in Hollywood when my engagement wasn't announced to one man or another.

Tallulah Bankhead, actor

I've done everything in the theatre except marry the property man.

Fanny Brice, comedian

Rock Hudson [is] the only man I know who can answer 'yes' or 'no' (and not a word more) to questions like 'how many films have you made?'

Jean Rook, journalist

Miss Welch tottered by, clad in a brown jersey dress that appeared to be on the inside of her skin.

Actor Maureen Lipman on Raquel Welch

Mamie [Van Doren] often acted like Mr Ed the Talking Horse and some say she was the forerunner of the Farrah Fawcett school of acting.

Paula Yates, TV presenter

Dramatic art in her opinion is knowing how to fill a sweater.

Actor Bette Davis on Jayne Mansfield

[Tony Curtis] only said that about 'kissing Hitler' because I wore prettier dresses than he did.

Marilyn Monroe, actor

It's a new low for actresses when you have to wonder what's between her ears instead of her legs.

Actor Katherine Hepburn on Sharon Stone

I think the measure of your success to a certain extent will be the amount of things written about you that aren't true.

Cybill Shepherd, actor

I think people can tell that we're not up our own bottoms.

Melanie B, singer

God ... what is normal? Is it normal to work in McDonalds? Is it normal to be a star?

K.D. Lang, singer-songwriter

I'm glad you like my Catherine. I like her too. She ruled thirty million people and had three thousand lovers. I do the best I can in two hours.

Actor Mae West, her speech from the stage following her performance in Catherine the Great

What I like about Hollywood is that one can get along by knowing two words of English – SWELL and LOUSY.

Vicki Baum, novelist

Suicide is much easier and more acceptable in Hollywood than growing old gracefully.

Julie Burchill, journalist

I don't know which came first, the chicken or the egg? Were the people satanic and the media just reported on that?

Lily Tomlin, comedian

I seem to live permanently in some kind of godawful soap opera.

Liz Hurley, actor

Television has no regard for the absence of talent: it merely makes you 'famous'.

Joanna Lumley, actor

I'm lucky that people have a negative conception of me: I can only look nice after that.

Sarah Ferguson, former Duchess of York

In America it's about how you're seen. In Australia it's about how you feel. Here, it's more important to appear to be nice than to have a heart.

Actor Rachel Griffiths on the British media

What's nice about my dating life is that I don't have to leave my house. All I have to do is read the paper: I'm marrying Richard Gere, dating Daniel Day-Lewis … and even Robert De Niro was in there for a day.

Julia Roberts, actor

People think I'm some sort of strange Teletubby.

Bjork, singer-songwriter

What does it mean when people applaud? …
Should I give 'em money? Say thank you? Lift my
dress? The 'lack' of applause – *that* I can respond to.

Barbra Streisand, actor and singer

It's just fashion, isn't it? Being a Scot and a lesbian
are two big handy ticks next to my name right now.

Ali Smith, novelist

······· Politics ····································

In this country American means white. Everybody
else has to hyphenate.

Toni Morrison, writer

If you think you're too small to have an impact, try
going to bed with a mosquito.

Anita Roddick, founder of The Body Shop

The common good is usually not very.

Fran Lebowitz, writer and humorist

Every society honours its live conformists and its
dead troublemakers.

Mignon McLaughlin, writer

The only possible way there'd be an uprising in this country would be if they banned car boot sales and caravanning.

Victoria Wood, comedian

Ninety-eight per cent of adults in this country are decent, hard-working honest Americans. It's the other two per cent that get all the publicity. But then, we elected them.

Lily Tomlin, comedian

My hope is that gays will be running the world, because then there would be no more war. Just a greater emphasis on military apparel.

Roseanne, comedian

If voting changed anything, they'd make it illegal.

Emma Goldman, political activist

I don't think you ever manage to deal with politics. You just cope with it.

Zola Budd, former athlete

If it's natural to kill, how come men have to go into training to learn how?

Joan Baez, singer-songwriter

I'm back ... and you knew I was coming. On my way here I passed a cinema with the sign 'The Mummy Returns'.

Margaret Thatcher, former British Prime Minister

What would bug a guy from the Taliban more than seeing a gay woman in a suit surrounded by Jews?

Ellen DeGeneres, comedian

Outside of the killings, Washington has one of the lowest crime rates in the country.

Marion Barry, former Mayor of Washington

What right does Congress have to go around making laws just because they deem it necessary?

Marion Barry, former Mayor of Washington

If a politician murders his mother, the first response of the press or of his opponents will likely be not that it was a terrible thing to do, but rather that in a statement made six years before he had gone on record as being opposed to matricide.

Meg Greenfield, journalist

Everyone should have a Willy.

Former Prime Minister Margaret Thatcher about Willy Whitelaw

There ain't no answer. There ain't gonna be any answer. There never has been an answer. That's the answer.

Gertrude Stein, writer

A diplomat is a person who can tell you to go to hell in such a way that you actually look forward to the trip.

Caskie Stinnett, writer and humorist

To wear your heart on your sleeve isn't a very good plan; you should wear it inside, where it functions best.

Margaret Thatcher, former British Prime Minister

A world without nuclear weapons would be less stable and more dangerous for all of us.

Margaret Thatcher, former British Prime Minister

Every middle-class person in America is on Prozac. Every poor person in America is on crack. Every middle-class person who is on Prozac has tremendous contempt for the poor person on crack.

Fran Lebowitz, writer and humorist

In my heart, I think a woman has two choices: either she's a feminist or a masochist.

Gloria Steinem, writer

In many languages, there is a single word for 'wife' and 'woman'. Perhaps we should be thankful that English is no longer one of them.

Dr Susan Maushart, Australian writer

Beware the bearded academic feminist. They'll have you washing up the wok while they read Marx with a glass of rough red.

Mandy Saloman, writer

I want women to be liberated and still be able to have a nice ass and shake it.

Shirley MacLaine, actor and writer

Standing in the middle of the road is very dangerous; you get knocked down by traffic from both sides.

Margaret Thatcher, former British Prime Minister

George W. Bush's email address is *president@whitehouse.gov*. When you email him, they send you back these wonderful messages, like 'President Bush will consider your email'. Will he shit, he won't even see it. But then they know where your computer is and you're on their hit list.

A.L. Kennedy, Scottish author

You can no more win a war than you can win an earthquake.

Jeannette Rankin, former US politician

The first victory is the avoidance of war.

Indira Gandhi, former Prime Minister of India

I don't want to pay money for the shit heads who are buying armaments around the world. Every time a missile goes overhead I look up and think, 'I bought the wing.'

Erica Jong, writer

There are two kinds of imperialists – imperialists and bloody imperialists.

Rebecca West, writer

Places

Melbourne is the kind of town that really makes you consider the question 'Is there life before death?'

Bette Midler, actor and singer

Are we going to Lebanon? I've never been there. I've been to Debenhams lots of times, though.

Melanie C, singer

Chernobyl looked nice in the brochure.

Victoria Wood, comedian

In this country there are only two seasons: winter and winter.

Shelagh Delaney, referring to England

… these English … you make one perfectly normal request at a normal volume and they pucker their rectums.

Dawn French, Jennifer Saunders and Ruby Wax

The great and recurrent question about abroad is, is it worth getting there?

Rose Macaulay, novelist

Y'all are so cute and y'all talk so proper over here. I love England.

Beyonce Knowles, pop singer

I miss New York. I still love how people talk to you on the street – just assault you and tell you what they think of your jacket.

Madonna, pop diva

The sun shone all day, but the people were boring as hell.

Actor Kim Catrall on California

Getting all wrought-up seldom helps except, of course, in Latin countries.

Alice-Leone Moats, humour writer

A private railroad car is not an acquired taste. One takes to it immediately.

Eleanor Robson Belmont, actor and writer

All creative people should be required to leave California for three months every year.

Gloria Swanson, actor

Unfortunately, there's a big anti-intellectual strain in the American south, and there always has been. We're not big on thought.

Donna Tartt, novelist

In Tulsa, restaurants have signs that say, 'Sorry, we're open.'

Roseanne, comedian

I had to move to New York for health reasons. I'm very paranoid and New York is the only place where my fears are justified.

Anita Wise, comedian

New York: The only city where people make radio requests like, 'This is for Tina – I'm sorry I stabbed you.'

Carol Leifer, writer and comedian

Even thin people look fat there.

Comedian Roseanne on New York

For some reason, a glaze passes over people's faces when you say 'Canada'.

Sondra Gottlieb, US ambassador's wife

When it's three o'clock in New York, it's still 1938 in London.

Bette Midler, actor and singer

English men. Charm the knickers off you with their mellow vowels and frivolous verbiage, and then, once they'd got them off, panic and run.

Margaret Atwood, novelist

I'd never heard of sticking gerbils up your ass before I came here.

Lucy Ellmann, novelist

A Frenchman is a German with good food.

Fran Lebowitz, writer and humorist

I have yet to meet a Frenchman who does not consider himself my superior.

Elizabeth Forsythe Hailey, novelist

I like Frenchmen very much, because even when they insult you they do it so nicely.

Josephine Baker, jazz singer

They tell me Saint-Tropez is uninhabitable this year. You only find people whose photographs appear in *Vogue*.

Colette, novelist

Being broke in London is miserable, but being broke in Paris is quite nice.

Kristin Scott Thomas, actor

At home a forty-five-year-old widow is considered old; in Italy she is merely regarded as ripe.

Elizabeth Forsythe Hailey, novelist

It is better to go there with a lover because otherwise frustrations may set in.

Actor and writer Ilka Chase on Venice

I always feel you can do Europe in a wheelchair.

Erma Bombeck, writer and humorist

Russia's a little bit like a critically ill patient. You have to get up every day and take the pulse and hope that nothing catastrophic happened the night before.

Condoleezza Rice, US presidential advisor

Body and Soul

···Sport and Fitness···

Men who have a thirty-six-televised-football-games-a-week-habit should be declared legally dead and their estates probated.

Erma Bombeck, writer and humorist

Men hate to lose. I once beat my husband at tennis. I asked him, 'Are we going to have sex again?' He said 'Yes, but not with each other.'

Rita Rudner, comedian

Weight-lifting apparatus is a curious phenomenon – machines invented to replicate the back-breaking manual labour the industrial revolution relieved us of.

Sue Grafton, novelist

I was a ballerina. I had to quit after I injured a groin muscle. It wasn't mine.

Rita Rudner, comedian

Body and Soul

I don't know much about football. I know what a goal is, which is surely the main thing about football.

Victoria Beckham, singer

Give a man a fish and he eats for the day. Teach him how to fish and you get rid of him all weekend.

Zenna Schaffer, writer

The Stronger Women Get, The More Men Love Football.

Mariah Burton Nelson – book title

The first time I see a jogger smiling, I'll consider it.

Joan Rivers, comedian

Men are not as interesting at my age as women. They are playing that game you play before you die: golf.

Anita Roddick, founder of The Body Shop

···· Death and Dying ··········

If I had any decency, I'd be dead. Most of my friends are.

Dorothy Parker, writer and wit

Death is just so there right now. It's Linda. It's Gianni and Diana.

Sue Margolis, novelist

Hospitals generally prefer people not to die in them. It disturbs the other patients and depresses the nurses.

Germaine Greer, feminist writer and academic

Canadians are cold so much of the time that many of them leave instructions to be cremated.

Cynthia Nelms, writer

And when you die, have everything buried with you. If the next wife wants it, make her dig. I'm going to have a mausoleum. More closet space.

Joan Rivers, comedian

My dream is to die in a tub of ice cream, with Mel Gibson.

Joan Rivers, comedian

I don't feel I really belong to this life. I am hovering like a seagull.

Isak Dinesen, writer

Body and Soul

If I weren't cremated, I'd leave all the useful bits of my body to science – except my thighs because nobody would want those.

Olivia Goldsmith, novelist and scriptwriter

Life without a body to put in it can't be much fun.

Caitlin Thomas, journalist

I think reincarnation is possible. Hopefully, we all get recycled.

Christina Ricci, actor

Hell looks like the girls' gym at my high school. In hell, I am taking gym, but I also have a book due.

Fran Lebowitz, writer and humorist

My heaven will be filled with wonderful young men and dukes.

Barbara Cartland, novelist

·····Religion·····························

When I look back on the fantastic mess of my life, my one hope is that God can make something of it.

Antonia White, writer

You can safely assume that you've created God in your own image when it turns out that God hates all the same people you do.

Anne Lamott, novelist

Men don't get cellulite. God might just be a man.

Rita Rudner, comedian

I was fired from [the convent], finally, for a lot of things, among them my insistence that the Immaculate Conception was spontaneous combustion.

Dorothy Parker, writer and wit

Faith is putting all your eggs in God's basket, then counting your blessings before they hatch.

Ramona C. Carroll, writer

Body and Soul

We feminists are supposed to have a problem with Mary – the pristine, perfect image of womanhood who makes the rest of us look like sin-drenched slappers.

Julie Burchill, journalist

Personally I blame the Virgin Mary. She was too passive! If only she had been more assertive ... turned round to God and said: 'No! Piss off ... I'm sorry but I'm not that kind of virgin! ... I'm saving myself for Buddha.'

Rhonda Carling-Rodgers, comedian

I wonder if other dogs think poodles are members of a weird religious cult.

Rita Rudner, comedian

Artistic Life

No writer should ever sleep with, live with or, God forbid, marry an aspiring writer – not without reading what happened to J.D. Salinger.

Amanda Craig, novelist

Finding a businessman interested in the arts is like finding chicken shit among the chicken salad.

Alice Neel, artist

I've given my memoirs far more thought than any of my marriages. You can't divorce a book.

Gloria Swanson, actor

If I want to be alone, some place I can write, I can read, I can pray, I can cry, I can do whatever I want – I go to the bathroom.

Alicia Keys, actor

For 15 years, I've been playing the same character – which is myself – and I'm bored with 'myself'.

Elle MacPherson, model

Playing is the only place where I've felt in touch with my sexuality, my spirituality and my emotions, and never ever, ever anywhere else. So my life is a bit tricky because when I'm not playing, I'm just trying to walk down the street.

Tori Amos, singer

Good art is in the wallet of the beholder.

Kathy Lette, writer

Body and Soul

The most important thing in acting is to be able to laugh and cry. If I have to cry, I think of my sex life. If I have to laugh, I think of my sex life.

Glenda Jackson, actor and Member of Parliament

Andy Warhol made fame more famous.

Fran Lebowitz, writer and humorist

Very few people possess true artistic ability. It is therefore both unseemly and unproductive to irritate the situation by making an effort. If you have a burning, restless urge to write or paint, simply eat something sweet and the feeling will pass.

Fran Lebowitz, writer and humorist

Hiring someone to write your autobiography is like paying someone to take a bath for you.

Mae West, actor

So, where's the Cannes Film Festival being held this year?

Christina Aguilera, singer

Everyone told me to pass on *Speed* because it was a 'bus movie'.

Sandra Bullock, actor

Everything makes me nervous – except making films.

Elizabeth Taylor, actor

I can do to him whatever I like. I'm allowed to torture him as much as I want. He's mine.

Novelist J.K. Rowling on Harry Potter

When you write happy endings you are not taken seriously as a writer.

Carol Shields, novelist

Write the truth and no one believes you: it's too alarming. So you might as well make it up.

Fay Weldon, writer

People may say that they don't like your novel, but they can't say you 'got it wrong'.

Victoria Glendinning, writer

It reached a point where I had to pretend I didn't know how to iron or I'd never have written anything at all.

Elizabeth Jane Howard, novelist

Body and Soul

I cannot imagine an occupation more in conflict with writing than homemaking.

Paulette Childress White, writer

If somebody could write a book for the people who never read they would make a fortune.

Nancy Mitford, writer

I am the only author with two hundred virgins in print.

Barbara Cartland, novelist

A person who publishes a book wilfully appears before the populace with his pants down.

Edna St Vincent Millay, poet

Americans look at you very differently, respect you greatly more when you write a book. It doesn't even matter if it's good.

Martha Stewart, cookery and style guru

The best kind of fame is a writer's fame. Just enough to get a good table at a restaurant and not enough for someone to interrupt you while you are eating.

Fran Lebowitz, writer and humorist

I'm a lousy writer; a helluva lot of people have got lousy taste.

Grace Metalious, novelist

Erotica is to porn what a crocheted cover is to a toilet roll: deeply naff.

Julie Burchill, journalist

Feminist porn's absurd. I'm totally against it. I like regular porn.

Camille Paglia, academic

I believe in censorship. I made a fortune out of it.

Mae West, actor

I've been making a comeback but nobody ever tells me where I've been.

Billie Holiday, jazz singer

I had to get rich in order to sing like I'm poor again.

Dolly Parton, singer-songwriter

I'm not sure where the notes come from sometimes. In the studio I'm like: 'I hope you save that, 'cos it ain't coming out any time again today.' Maybe they could get a dolphin in.

Mariah Carey, singer

Body and Soul

The worst frustration for a singer is choosing a career in making music and then not being able to make music because you're always giving interviews.

Shakira, singer

Pop music is the natural habitat of the supremely superficial.

Kirsty McColl, singer-singwriter

I saw my first porno film recently – a Jewish porno film – one minute of sex and nine minutes of guilt.

Joan Rivers, comedian

I'm an actor! An actress is someone who wears boa feathers.

Sigourney Weaver, actor

I feel a bit guilty making such a good living out of something that I enjoy so much. Paid to dress up, pretend to be somebody, have all my friends around me, being part of a big gang, shouting and misbehaving ...

Dawn French, comedian

If I'd been clever, I'd have been a sociologist or something, but I wasn't, so I became an actress.

Kristin Scott Thomas, actor

Film actors really do believe that lazing around a trailer all day having pancake applied until the time comes to utter one line is up there, physically and mentally, with coal mining in the 1800s.

Barbara Ellen, journalist

The more flesh you show, the higher up the ladder you go.

Kim Basinger, actor

Status

I never realised until lately that women were supposed to be the inferior sex.

Katherine Hepburn, actor

I, along with the critics, have never taken myself very seriously.

Elizabeth Taylor, actor

I don't live well in a confined state.

Nicole Kidman, actor

My whole career has been an act of revenge.

Ruby Wax, comedian

Body and Soul

Unfortunately, sometimes people don't hear you until you scream.

Stefanie Powers, actor

If it's a woman, it's caustic; if it's a man, it's authoritative

Barbara Walters, journalist

Being powerful is like being a lady. If you have to tell people you are, you aren't.

Margaret Thatcher, former British Prime Minister

The secret of getting ahead is getting started.

Sally Berger, writer

Some of us are becoming the men we wanted to marry.

Gloria Steinem, feminist writer

Besides Shakespeare and me, who do you think there is?

Gertrude Stein, writer

What I wanted to be when I grew up was – in charge.

Wilma Vaught, Brigadier General of the US Air Force

Status

My fame has enabled me to torture more formidable men.

Sharon Stone, actor

Ultimately, the lower middle classes are the most deviant. That's why they have net curtains; they have things to hide, the weirdos.

Jenny Éclair, comedian

The thing women have got to learn is that nobody gives you power. You just take it.

Roseanne, comedian

Remember, *I'm* the leading lady.

Actor Julie Andrews to Rock Hudson

Sometimes you have to be a bitch to get things done.

Madonna, pop diva

I found my inner-bitch and ran with her.

Courtney Love, rock singer

If I were well-behaved, I'd die of boredom.

Tallulah Bankhead, actor

Body and Soul

I think it's about time we voted for senators with breasts. After all, we've been voting for boobs long enough.

Claire Sargent, US politician

····· Motherhood ·····················

Next time I'm not just having an epidural for the birth – I'm having one for the conception as well.

Sally James, comedian

If men had to have babies, they would only ever have one.

Diana, Princess of Wales

Every four weeks I go up a bra size … it's worth being pregnant just for the breasts.

Natasha Hamilton, pop singer

It [giving birth] was easier than having a tattoo.

Nicole Appleton, pop singer

Do you think those triplets were really mine? After all, I did only go into hospital to have my ears pierced.

Victoria Wood, comedian

Up until they go to school, they're relatively portable.

Liz Hurley, actor

The English hate children. They keep their dogs at home and send their kids off to high-class kennels, called Eton and Harrow.

Kathy Lette, writer

If they really wanted to lower the number of teenage pregnancies, they would pay women who've had a couple of kids to visit secondary schools and demonstrate their varicose veins, stretch marks and piles.

Jenny Éclair, comedian

If pregnancy were a book they would cut the last two chapters.

Nora Ephron, writer and humorist

Giving birth is like taking your lower lip and forcing it over your head.

Carole Burnett, comedian

A lot of women I know believe in natural childbirth. Just thinking about the pain makes me want to take drugs.

Ellen DeGeneres, comedian

Body and Soul

Babies are born looking like the ugliest relative on his side of the family.

Jenny Éclair, comedian

They're all mine ... Of course, I'd trade any of them for a dishwasher.

Comedian Roseanne on her children

We spent the first twelve months of our children's lives teaching them to walk and talk and the next twelve telling them to sit down and shut up.

Phyllis Diller, comedian

Experts say you should never hit your children in anger. When is a good time? When you're feeling festive?

Roseanne, comedian

Always be nice to your children because they are the ones who will choose your rest home.

Phyllis Diller, comedian

The four basic guilt groups – food, love, mom and work – are still going strong.

Cathy Guisewite, cartoonist

My mother could make anybody feel guilty – she used to get letters of apology from people she didn't even know.

Joan Rivers, comedian

The best way to keep children at home is to make the home atmosphere pleasant – and let the air out of their tyres.

Dorothy Parker, writer and wit

I don't approve of smacking – I just use a cattle prod.

Jenny Éclair, comedian

Let's face it, if God had meant men to have children, he would have given them PVC aprons.

Victoria Wood, comedian

I knew I was an unwanted child when I saw that my bath toys were a toaster and a radio.

Joan Rivers, comedian

If you want your children to listen, try talking softly – to someone else.

Ann Landers, writer

Body and Soul

It goes without saying that you should never have more children than you have car windows.

Erma Bombeck, writer and humorist

The real menace in dealing with a five-year-old is that in no time at all you begin to sound like a five-year-old.

Jean Kerr, playwright

Whenever my mother sees me she says, 'Jenny, Jenny, why aren't you wearing a petticoat?'
'Mother, it's because I've got jeans on.'

Jenny Éclair, comedian

My husband knows so much about rearing children that I've suggested he has the next one and I'll sit back and give advice.

Diana, Princess of Wales

Hey, the way I figure it is this: if the kids are still alive by the time my husband comes home, I've done my job.

Roseanne, comedian

They say men can never experience the pain of childbirth ... they can if you hit them in the goolies with a cricket bat ... for fourteen hours.

Jo Brand, comedian

I realise why women die in childbirth – it's preferable.

Sherry Glaser, actor

Of course, the placenta is very useful because it is so very hideous that by comparison, the baby is quite attractive.

Jenny Éclair, comedian

To simulate the birth experience, take one car jack, insert into rectum, pump to maximum height and replace with jack hammer. And that would be a good birth.

Kathy Lette, writer

The children never forgave me. Oedipus only killed his father and married his mother, but I sold their Nintendo.

Sue Arnold, writer

We have made mistakes with our children, which will undoubtedly become clearer as they get old enough to write their own books.

Jean Kerr, playwright

Having children accentuates more marital faults than adultery does.

Julie Burchill, journalist

One of the reasons children are such duds socially is that they say things like 'When do you think you're going to be dead, Grandma?'

Jean Kerr, playwright

I think children shouldn't be seen or heard.

Jo Brand, comedian

Even when freshly washed and relieved of all obvious confections, children tend to be sticky. One can only assume this has something to do with not smoking enough.

Fran Lebowitz, writer and humorist

···· # Food and Drink ············

Never eat more than you can lift.

Miss Piggy, porcine sex symbol

One more drink and I'll be under the host.

Dorothy Parker, writer and wit

I tried not drinking once. I heard myself talking all night and then, worse than that, next day I had total recall. It was terrifying.

Jennifer Saunders, comedian

I worry about scientists discovering that lettuce has been fattening all along.

Erma Bombeck, writer and humorist

I like anything that comes under the heading, 'It's got calories and you can put it in your mouth.'

Jo Brand, comedian

French fries. I love them. Some people are chocolate and sweets people. I love French fries. That and caviar.

Cameron Diaz, actor

Psychologists argue that eating disorders are caused by upbringing – specifically the bringing up of your lunch.

Debbie Barham, comedy writer

Come up to me with a doughnut or a bag of chips. That would be perfect.

Emma Bunton, pop singer

If you want to know the truth about actresses, it's that we're hungry all the time. We really don't eat. We live on Muesli bars and yoghurt.

Julianne Moore, actor

Body and Soul

Beware of the man who loves his mother's macaroni and cheese more than he loves sex. Or you. Or anything.

Linda Stasi, journalist

One of my worst moments was when I drank my finger-dipping bowl at a royal party. I thought it was soup. Not only did I drink it, I also asked for the recipe.

Tara Palmer-Tomkinson, 'It' girl

Any dish that tastes good with capers in it, tastes even better with capers not in it.

Nora Ephron, writer and humorist

A food is not necessarily essential just because your child hates it.

Katherine Whitehorn, journalist

I hate salad. I put mushrooms in them because there is nothing in them, they're totally empty, like Britney Spears' head.

Joan Rivers, comedian

You could probably get through life without knowing how to roast a chicken, but the question is, would you want to?

Nigella Lawson, food writer

Men like to barbecue. Men will cook if danger is involved.

Rita Rudner, comedian

Everything you see I owe to spaghetti.

Sophia Loren, actor

My mother is such a lousy cook that Thanksgiving at her house is a time of sorrow.

Rita Rudner, comedian

It's OK for old people to drink really heavily at night, because they can go up to bed on that electric chair thing attached to the staircase.

Rhona Cameron, comedian

Ask your child what he wants for dinner only if he's buying.

Fran Lebowitz, writer and humorist

Body and Soul

[In his fridge] I found yogurt whose expiry date read 'When Dinosaurs Roamed the Earth'.

Kathy Lette, writer

The name Big Mac is generally supposed to have come about because it is a big McDonald's burger, but in fact it was named after a big raincoat whose taste it so closely resembles.

Jo Brand, comedian

I can't see the point in making tons of food if people are just going to sit there and eat it.

Jenny Éclair, comedian

Don't take any recipe on faith. There are some hostile recipes in this world.

Peg Bracken, food writer

A lot of men get very funny about women drinking: they don't really like it. Well, I'm sorry, lads, but if we didn't get pissed, most of you would never get a shag.

Jenny Éclair, comedian

Coffee in England always tastes like a chemistry experiment.

Agatha Christie, crime writer

I have dieted continuously for the last two decades and lost a total of seven hundred and fifty-eight pounds. By all calculations, I should be hanging from a charm bracelet.

Erma Bombeck, writer and humorist

I've lost the same half-stone so many times my cellulite's got déjà vu … I don't need a diet. What I need is a tapeworm.

Sue Margolis, novelist

I got my figure back after giving birth. Sad, I'd hoped to get somebody else's.

Caroline Quentin, actor

Are the rich the new poor with their horrible mucked-about food, where nothing is allowed to look or taste of itself?

Sue Townsend, writer

······ Childhood ························

My dad said to me, on Christmas: 'You were the ugliest child the hospital had ever seen. When we took you home they gave us two blankets – one to put over your head.'

Barbara Ellen, journalist

I don't think I remember my first memory.

Ellen DeGeneres, comedian

If I had a family motto, it would be Do What You Want, You Will Anyway.

Tama Janowitz, writer

[My parents] had me absolutely convinced that I might not be able to have a hamburger in Woolworth's in Birmingham, but I could be president of the United States, if I wanted to be, and probably ought to be, from their point of view.

Condoleezza Rice, US presidential advisor

School was a bitch for me.

Cher, singer and actor

Think what a better world it would be if we all, the

whole world, had cookies and milk about three
o'clock every afternoon and then lay down on our
blankets for a nap.

Barbara Jordan, US politician

People always ask me, 'Were you funny as a child?'
Well, no, I was an accountant.

Ellen DeGeneres, comedian

I was brought up in a very tough Catholic school. I
was expelled for not smoking.

Rhonda Carling-Rodgers, comedian

I left school at fifteen having passed only one test –
my cervical smear test.

Kathy Lette, writer

When I was in school they showed us a sex
education film about a boy calling up a girl on the
phone and asking her out on a date. Nowadays I'm
sure they show *Nine and a Half Weeks* or something
starring Sharon Stone.

Ellen DeGeneres, comedian

It is a prerogative of youth to be in a mess all the
time.

Vicki Baum, writer

My mother always told me I wouldn't amount to anything because I procrastinate. I said, 'Just wait.'

Judy Tenuta, comedian

Your twenties are crap! They are exhausting. Because you're dancing for ten years. But I'm so tired, I want to go home. But I can't, I'm in my twenties. I've got to stay out and drink and take more drugs, and pretend I'm having fun with people I don't like. I just want to go home and read the Habitat catalogue.

Rhona Cameron, comedian

······ Health ······

We're medically designed to laugh at ourselves because otherwise we wouldn't be able to fart – if the human race didn't fart we probably wouldn't have a sense of humour. It's a sort of a design fault.

Jenny Éclair, comedian

There is no such thing as inner peace. There is only nervousness or death.

Fran Lebowitz, writer and humorist

One out of four people in this country is mentally unbalanced. Think of your three closest friends – and if they seem OK then you're the one!

Ann Landers, writer

Neurotics are always looking for something to overdo.

Mignon McLaughlin, writer

On a good day I think I'm a relatively sane person with a few frayed wires. On a bad day I think 'Just lock me up.'

Rosie O'Donnell, TV presenter

'So what?' you may think. 'My obsessions might be a bit unrealistic, but at least they keep life perky. I mean, what else do I have to do with my time, take up needlepoint?'

Cynthia Heimel, writer

It worries me that people see pain as an alien thing There won't be any poetry written soon if everyone's on an even keel.

Susan Sarandon, actor

One should only see a psychiatrist out of boredom.

Muriel Spark, novelist

Body and Soul

Even if I read about a disease and it says, 'This disease is present only in seventy-year-old Asian men', I feel, Oh! I could be the first white woman to have this disease.

Fran Lebowitz, writer and humorist

Warning: Humour may be hazardous to your illness.

Ellie Katz, scientist and 'playologist'

Hysteria, like everything else, comes with practice.

Caitlin Thomas, journalist

Women complain about premenstrual syndrome, but I think of it as the only time of the month that I can be myself.

Roseanne, comedian

A male gynaecologist is like an auto mechanic who never owned a car.

Carrie Snow, comedian

I love to go to the doctor. Where else would a man look at me and say, 'Take off your clothes?'

Phyllis Diller, comedian

Health

Whoever thought up the word 'Mammogram'?
Every time I hear it, I think I'm supposed to put my
breast in an envelope and send it to someone.

Jan King, novelist

I have a very low threshold of pain. Not even a
limbo dancer could get down there.

Kathy Lette, writer

Doctors and nurses are people who give you
medicine until you die.

Deborah Martin, novelist

Some of my worst enemies have been doctors.

Rebecca West, novelist

Once you've cured this and cured that, if you're
making money out of ill people you're going to
have to produce more ill people to keep going.

Margaret Atwood, novelist

To put private enterprise into the idea of health
care is a heinous crime! Much better waste it! Let it
be frittered away! Let a bunch of dopes lose it!

Fran Lebowitz, writer and humorist

Body and Soul

Research shows that the common cold is ... so common you wouldn't be out of line to call it a floozy.

Ellen DeGeneres, comedian

No one would be foolish enough to say an ulcer is contagious, but almost everybody who has an ulcer got it from somebody, usually a relative or business associate.

Ann Landers, writer

Things you don't want to hear during liposuction:
1. 'Accept this sacrifice, oh Lord Beelzebub!'
2. 'Hey! Who's got the camera? Get a load of this freak of nature!'
3. 'So everyone's washed their hands right? No? Well just wipe them on your overalls – that'll do.'

Anonymous

Decades of nurses – mostly women – have come up with their own acronyms to describe annoying patients and doctors – mostly men – in a way that neither could know about:
a. D&D: Divorced and Desperate (middle-aged female who visits doctor weekly just for male attention)
b. Metabolic clinic: the tea room
c. PRATFO: Patient Reassured And Told to F*** Off

d. Scratch and sniff: gynaecological examination
e. Slashers: general surgeons
f. VTMK: Voice To Melt Knickers (the voice deliberately cultivated by some doctors)
g. Woolly jumper: any non-acute physician

Sex and Other Laughing Matters

Sex

'Sex,' she says, 'is a subject like any other subject. Every bit as interesting as agriculture.'

Muriel Spark, novelist

The grass is always greener on the other side of the fence. So if you don't want to stain your skirt, do it on this side.

Joan Rivers, comedian

Last night I asked my husband, 'What's you favourite sexual position?' and he replied, 'Next door.'

Joan Rivers, comedian

I'm old-fashioned. I like it when a man pays … for sex.

Wendy Liebman, comedian

Sex and Other Laughing Matters

If I was the Virgin Mary, I would have said no.

Stevie Smith, poet

I blame my mother for my poor sex life. All she told me was, 'the man goes on top and the woman underneath'. For three years my husband and I slept on bunk beds.

Joan Rivers, comedian

My ultimate fantasy is to entice a man to my bedroom, put a gun to his head and say, 'Make babies or die.'

Ruby Wax, comedian

I may look sweet but I wear leather underwear.

Emma Bunton, pop singer

Women are like ovens. We need 5 to 15 minutes to heat up.

Sandra Bullock, actor

Personally I know nothing about sex because I've always been married.

Zsa Zsa Gabor, actor

After lovemaking, do you,
a. Go to sleep?
b. Light a cigarette?
c. Return to the front of the bus?

Joan Rivers, comedian

He claims to be a great sexual athlete, just because he always comes first.

Ellie Laine, comedian

That's definitely the trouble with upper-class Englishmen – they just can't drive past a perversion without pulling over.

Kathy Lette, writer

Men love any underwear that's easy to get off.

Jo Brand, comedian

Men who tell you they read the 'Ann Summers' catalogue for the articles are lying.

Rita Rudner, comedian

I'd get into bondage, but there are too many strings attached.

Donna Gephart, journalist

Sex and Other Laughing Matters

It's been so long since I made love, I can't even remember who gets tied up.

Joan Rivers, comedian

I sometimes think that what men really want now is a sexually experienced virgin.

Anonymous

The young always think that they invented sex and somehow hold full literary rights on the subject.

Mary Wesley, novelist

When mom found my diaphragm, I told her it was a bathing cap for my cat.

Liz Winston, comedian

If sex is such a natural phenomenon, how come there are so many books on how to?

Bette Midler, actor and singer

After we made love he took a piece of chalk and made an outline of my body.

Joan Rivers, comedian

The female orgasm is more of a mystery than the continued career success of George W. Bush.

Kathy Lette, writer

Most men would probably prefer to swallow the post-coital cigarette than hear an honest answer to: 'Was that good for you?'

Barbara Ellen, journalist

Grab the penis, it breaks the ice, it's kind of a fun friendly thing to do!

Cynthia Heimel, journalist

Shopping is better than sex. At least if you're not satisfied, you can exchange it for something you really like.

Adrienne E. Gusoff, writer and teacher

I could never be comfortable at an orgy. I'd always be thinking there would be someone making rabbit ears behind my back.

Diane Nichols, comedian

Don't criticise in the sack. Discuss constructively later.

Dr Ruth Westheimer, sex therapist

Sex and Other Laughing Matters

When the grandmothers of today hear the word 'Chippendales', they don't necessarily think of chairs.

Jean Kerr, playwright

I never quite know what people mean when they brag about how they are like animals in bed. Which animal? A big scary tiger? A gerbil?

Barbara Ellen, journalist

When feeling cheap and nasty, remind yourself that without infidelity, literature and opera would be up shit creek.

Kathy Lette, writer

It's not that men fear intimacy ... it's that they're hypochondriacs of intimacy. They always think they have it when they don't.

Lorrie Moore, novelist

What's that useless piece of flesh at the end of a penis called? A man.

Graffiti

The fact is I am not having sex. But I feel absolutely ripe for the – what would you say – plucking?

Angelina Jolie, actor

Show me a frigid woman and, nine times out of ten, I'll show you a little man.

Julie Burchill, journalist

Beware of the man who denounces women writers; his penis is tiny and he cannot spell.

Erica Jong, novelist

Do we want one? Good God no! The day Freud came up with penis envy, I think his brains had to have been out to lunch.

Helen Gurley Brown, journalist

I mean if you were a bloke, would you put it in a mouth where there are teeth? The teeth of a female who's been discriminated against for centuries?

Kathy Lette, writer

Sex was for men, and marriage, like lifeboats, was for women and children.

Carrie Fisher, actor and writer

The truth was that with all my lipstick and mascara and curves, I was as unresponsive as a fossil … I used to lie awake at night wondering why the boys came after me.

Marilyn Monroe, actor

Phone sex is a growth industry these disease-conscious days. Through the miracle of modern technology, you can reach out and not touch someone.

Alice Kahn, scientist and writer

When I had my baby, I screamed and screamed. And that was just during the conception.

Joan Rivers, comedian

·····Relationships·····

Being in love with yourself means never having to say you've got a headache.

Ellie Laine, comedian

Only time can heal your broken heart, just as time can heal his broken arms and legs.

Miss Piggy, porcine sex symbol

Whenever I date a guy I think, is this the man I want my children to spend their weekends with?

Rita Rudner, comedian

If someone had told me years ago that sharing a sense of humour was so vital to partnerships, I could have avoided a lot of sex!

Kate Beckinsale, actor

I think, therefore I'm single.

Liz Winstead, comedian

You can always tell what kind of a person a man really thinks you are by the earrings he gives you.

Audrey Hepburn, actor

How many of you ever started dating someone because you were too lazy to commit suicide?

Judy Tenuta, comedian

What do you do when your boyfriend walks out? Shut the door.

Angela Martin, writer

Women leave relationships when they can't take it another minute. Men leave when they find someone better.

Justin Rosenholtz, comedian

Sex and Other Laughing Matters

Women might be able to fake orgasms. But men can fake whole relationships.

Sharon Stone, actor

I'm really demanding. No girl really wants just a guy. You want a prince, you want Jesus. So when he comes around and his name is Steve, what are you supposed to do?

Macy Gray, singer

I change my mind so much I need two boyfriends and a girlfriend.

Pink, rock singer

I can't be in a relationship, I ruin them all. I think I'm a lesbian.

Roseanne, comedian

My advice to young women is to find a partner who has grown up with older sisters. They consider women important and they do not see them as an alien race. When you sit next to them, they talk to you.

Anne Robinson, journalist

My mother said it was simple to keep a man, you must be a maid in the living room, a cook in the kitchen and a whore in the bedroom. I said I'd hire the first two and take care of the bedroom bit.

Jerry Hall, model

I was a complete tart before I met Norman.

Zoe Ball, TV and radio presenter

I wanted to make it really special on Valentine's day, so I tied my boyfriend up. And for three solid hours I watched whatever I wanted on TV.

Tracy Smith, comedian

I don't have a boyfriend right now. I'm looking for anyone with a job that I don't have to support.

Former model Anna Nicole Smith

Everything I buy is vintage and smells funny. Maybe that's why I don't have a boyfriend.

Lucy Liu, actor

Boyfriends have to understand my needs. I shower four times a day.

Anna Kournikova, tennis player and model

Sex and Other Laughing Matters

The historical St Valentine was clubbed to death you know.

Lynne Truss, writer

A kiss is a lovely trick designed by nature to stop speech when words become superfluous.

Ingrid Bergman, actor

Honestly, I like everything. Boyish girls, girlish boys, the thick, the thin. Which is a problem when I'm walking down the street.

Angelina Jolie, actor

How absurd and delicious it is to be in love with somebody younger than yourself. Everybody should try it.

Barbara Pym, writer

Love is much nicer to be in than an automobile accident, a tight girdle, a higher tax bracket or a holding pattern over Philadelphia.

Judith Viorst, poet

Of course I can get a man. Whenever I walk past a building site there are twenty guys shouting, 'Doing anything on Tuesday, love?'

Minnie Driver, actor

Relationships

It's like being in a room with eight Labradors
sniffing round you, and a Rottweiler who won't
come near you – I know which one I'm drawn to.

Tara Palmer-Tomkinson, 'It' girl

When we attempt to buy love the price goes up, as
with other commodities.

Ann Landers, writer

I've been on so many blind dates, I should get a free
dog.

Wendy Liebman, comedian

Once a woman has forgiven her man, she must not
reheat his sins for breakfast.

Marlene Dietrich, actor

Before I met my husband, I'd never fallen in love,
though I'd stepped in it a few times.

Rita Rudner, comedian

If it is your time love will track you down like a
cruise missile. If you say 'No! I don't want it right
now,' that's when you'll get it for sure.

Lynda Barry, cartoonist

Sex and Other Laughing Matters

Personally I think if a woman hasn't met the right man by the time she's twenty-four, she may be lucky.

Jean Kerr, playwright

Infidelity is reason enough for gun control.

Barbara Lazear Ascher, relationships writer

Kids are like husbands – they're fine as long as they're someone else's.

Marsha Warfield, comedian

Familiarity breeds attempt.

Jane Ace, radio entertainer

I'm at a point where I want a man in my life – but not in my house! Just come in, attach a VCR, and get out.

Joy Behar, comedian

Revenge is sweet. Sweeter than tiramisu.

Kathy Lette, writer

Women want mediocre men, and men are working hard to become as mediocre as possible.

Margaret Mead, anthropologist

When he's late for dinner, I know he's either having an affair or is lying dead in the street. I always hope it's the street.

Jessica Tandy, actor

I like to wake up feeling a new man.

Jean Harlow, actor

Honey, sex doesn't stop till you're in the grave.

Lena Horne, singer

If you're a woman living, you've been done wrong by a man.

Oprah Winfrey, TV presenter

I don't think men and women are meant to live together. They are totally different animals.

Diana Dors, actor

If you're a woman – and who isn't these days – you know where the real fight for equality and justice is taking place ... in the bathrooms of America.

Alice Kahn, scientist and writer

Sex and Other Laughing Matters

When a man can't explain a woman's actions, the first thing he thinks about is the condition of her uterus.

Clare Boothe Luce, author and diplomat

A woman without a man is like a neck without a pain.

Graffiti

'Strong Woman', used by men, means 'she can take it'. And if she can take it, why not do it to her again?

Julie Burchill, journalist

The way to a man's heart is through his heart and it helps if it hurts. Hurts him, not you.

Doris Lilly, writer

If love is the answer, can you rephrase the question?

Lily Tomlin, comedian

Love is something sent from Heaven to worry the hell out of you.

Dolly Parton, singer-songwriter

Sometimes I believe that some people are better at love than others, and sometimes I believe that everyone is faking it.

Nora Ephron, writer and humorist

Love is not merely blind but mentally afflicted.

Alice Thomas Ellis, journalist

You know, new lovers really should have a minimum isolation period of say, six months, so as not to nauseate absolutely everyone they meet.

Kathy Lette, writer

How could I be sleeping with this peculiar man ... Surely only true love could justify my lack of taste.

Margaret Atwood, novelist

I would hope I can attract both men and women. And that when a person is attracted to me, they're not thinking about my genitals.

K.D. Lang, singer-songwriter

No man wanted me. Rapists would tap me on the shoulder and say 'Seen any girls?'

Joan Rivers, comedian

Sex and Other Laughing Matters

Sometimes love doesn't come to us. We have to go out hunting. It's like pigs looking for truffles. It's called dating.

Patti LuPone, singer

You get all your boyfriends on sale. It's called Bargain Debasement.

Lorrie Moore, novelist

Never trust a man who says 'Don't struggle'.

Jenny Éclair, comedian

There are three kinds of kissers: the fire extinguisher, the mummy and the vacuum cleaner.

Helen Gurley Brown, journalist

'Women are like barnacles,' he said, 'they are always ready to fasten upon a wreck.'

Mary Braddon, novelist

Save a boyfriend for a rainy day. And another in case it doesn't rain.

Mae West, actor

Love wears a bumper sticker that says 'My other car is a hearse'.

Julie Burchill, journalist

Marriage

Married men inevitably say that their wives don't understand them, they haven't been sleeping together for ten years, they're not going to leave their wives until their children grow up and they've never felt this way about another woman. Women, who would otherwise laugh out loud at their friends were they to volunteer this same information, believe them.

Paula Yates, TV presenter

•••••• Marriage ••••••••••••••••••••

Not all women give most of their waking thoughts to the problem of pleasing men. Some are married.

Emma Lee, writer

When I got married, I said to my therapist, 'I want to do something creative.' He said, 'Why don't you have a baby?' I hope he's dead now.

Joy Behar, comedian

It's true that some couples have 'arrangements'. Usually, the husband arranges to have sex with other women, and the wife arranges to divorce him.

Barbara Ellen, journalist

185

Sex and Other Laughing Matters

Husbands are like fires – they go out if unattended.

Zsa Zsa Gabor, actor

More husbands would leave home if they knew
how to pack.

Anonymous

I've told Billy if I ever caught him cheating, I
wouldn't kill him because I love his children and
they need a dad. But I would beat him up. I know
where all of his sports injuries are.

Angelina Jolie, actor

In Hollywood a marriage is a success if it outlasts
milk.

Rita Rudner, comedian

I never married because there was no need. I have
three pets at home which answer the same purpose
as a husband. I have a dog which growls every
morning, a parrot which swears all afternoon, and a
cat that comes home late at night.

Marie Corelli, novelist

Marriage changes passion … suddenly you're in bed
with a relative.

Anonymous

I'd marry again if I found a man who had fifteen million dollars, would sign over half to me, and guarantee that he'd be dead within a year.

Bette Davis, actor

Any intelligent woman who reads the marriage contract, and then goes into it, deserves all the consequences.

Isadora Duncan, dancer

I don't believe in divorce. I believe in widowhood.

Carolyn Green, writer

A man in love is incomplete until he has married. Then he's finished.

Zsa Zsa Gabor, actor

Why does a woman work ten years to change a man's habits and then complain that he's not the man she married?

Barbra Streisand, actor and singer

Marriage is like a phone call in the night: first the ring, and then you wake up.

Evelyn Hendrickson, writer

Sex and Other Laughing Matters

If you want to sacrifice the admiration of many men for the criticism of one, go ahead, get married.

Katharine Hepburn, actor

Before marriage, a girl has to make love to a man to hold him. After marriage, she has to hold him to make love to him.

Marilyn Monroe, actor

I love being married. It's so great to find that one special person you want to annoy for the rest of your life.

Rita Rudner, comedian

Someone asked me why women don't gamble as much as men do, and I gave the commonsensical reply that we don't have as much money. That was a true and incomplete answer. In fact, women's total instinct for gambling is satisfied by marriage.

Gloria Steinem, feminist writer

Getting divorced just because you don't love a man is almost as silly as getting married just because you do.

Zsa Zsa Gabor, actor

One advantage of marriage is that, when you fall out of love with him or he falls out of love with you, it keeps you together until you fall in again.

Judith Viorst, poet

He's the kind of man a woman would have to marry to get rid of.

Mae West, actor

Changing husbands is only changing troubles.

Kathleen Norris, poet and novelist

Bigamy is when you're married to one man too many. Monogamy is the same thing.

Erica Jong, novelist

It should be a very happy marriage – they are both so much in love with him.

Irene Thomas, writer

Let's be honest – a wedding is absolutely the worst way to start married life.

Caitlin Moran, journalist

Sex and Other Laughing Matters

Marriage is what happens when one at least of the partners doesn't want the other to get away.

Fay Weldon, journalist

The average man looks on matrimony as a hitching post where he can tie a woman and leave her until he comes home nights.

Helen Rowland, writer

It was a mixed marriage. I'm human, he was a Klingon.

Carol Leifer, writer and comedian

I'm more afraid of marriage than death.

Shakira, singer

I don't know that I could have handled work, children and husband. Work and children I could have. But the husband was too much.

Diane von Furstenberg, designer

When you're young, you think of marriage as a train you simply have to catch. You run and run until you've caught it, and then you sit back and look out of the window and realise you're bored.

Elizabeth Bowen, novelist

I never wanted to get married. I felt it was a bad contract to get into.

Debbie Harry, rock singer

Ideally, couples need three lives; one for him, one for her, and one for them together.

Jaqueline Bisset, actor

It is absurd to suggest that a wife should be on 24-hour call like an inhalator squad – ready for romance at the drop of a hint.

Ann Landers, writer

We've just marked our tenth wedding anniversary on the calendar and threw darts at it.

Phyllis Diller, comedian

Historically, marrying for passion is a relatively new phenomenon – one that just happens to correspond with the rising divorce rate.

Hazel McClay, writer

I want a man who's kind and understanding. Is that too much to ask of a millionaire?

Zsa Zsa Gabor, actor

Sex and Other Laughing Matters

One wishes for marriage for one's daughter and, for one's descendants, better luck.

Fay Weldon, journalist

Hollywood is the only place in the world where an amicable divorce means each one gets fifty per cent of the publicity.

Lauren Bacall, actor

I sometimes think that being widowed is God's way of telling you to come off the pill.

Victoria Wood, comedian

Marriage used to be for the having and growing of children; now there are few marriages that can withstand the pressures of those events.

Erica Jong, novelist

Men who have pierced ears are better prepared for marriage. They've experienced pain and bought jewellery.

Rita Rudner, comedian

Now I'm free! And the man who caused me so much pain now says, 'I want to marry you.' And I say, 'Who doesn't?'

Oprah Winfrey, TV presenter

Married men have a habit of making even the most confident woman turn into something of a walking cliché.

Paula Yates, TV presenter

I've married a few people I shouldn't have, but haven't we all?

Mamie Van Doren, actor and model

I am nearly as keen on divorce as I am on shopping.

India Knight, journalist

There are men I could spend eternity with, but not this life.

Kathleen Norris, poet and novelist

I only knew one thing for sure. Marriage was definitely the chief cause of divorce.

Kathy Lette, writer

Get a job, your husband hates you. Get a good job, your husband leaves you. Get a stupendous job, you husband leaves you for a teenager.

Cynthia Heimel, journalist

Never give back the ring. Never. Swallow it first.

Joan Rivers, comedian

The wages of sin is alimony.

Carolyn Wells, writer

An archaeologist is the best husband any woman can have: the older she gets, the more interested he is in her.

Agatha Christie, crime writer

Opposites attract, but like is much easier to be married to.

Diana Douglas Darrid, actor

People keep asking me if I'll marry again. It's as if after you've had one car crash you want another.

Stephanie Beacham, actor

Did you read about the woman who stabbed her husband thirty-seven times? I admire her restraint.

Roseanne, comedian

Sometimes I wonder if men and women suit each other. Perhaps they should live next door and just visit now and then.

Katherine Hepburn, actor

Marriage is a great institution, but I'm not ready for an institution yet.

Mae West, actor

Never go to bed mad. Stay up and fight.

Phyllis Diller, comedian

Husbands are living proof that women have a sense of humour.

Anonymous

Don't marry a man to reform him – that's what reform schools are for.

Mae West, actor

I have yet to hear a man ask for advice on how to combine marriage and a career.

Gloria Steinem, feminist writer

Sex and Other Laughing Matters

We weren't meant to have futures. We were meant to marry them.

Nora Ephron, writer and wit

My mother was desperate to get me married. She used to say, 'Sure he's a murderer. But a single murderer.'

Joan Rivers, comedian

I still miss my ex-husband (but my aim is improving).

Anonymous

I'd like to marry a nice domesticated homosexual with a fetish for wiping down formica and different vacuum cleaner attachments.

Jenny Éclair, comedian

In our family we don't divorce our men – we bury them.

Ruth Gordon, actor and writer

Animals

There is nothing sadder than hearing someone talking to their cat as if it were a real human being with a brain and a Marks and Spencer's charge card.

Jenny Éclair, comedian

The only point in going to the zoo is to watch animals shag. Me, I'd boot out the giant pandas unless they started giving us our money's worth.

Jenny Éclair, comedian

If ants are such busy workers, how come they find the time to go to all the picnics?

Marie Dressler, actor and writer

If cats had slime or scales instead of fur there would be no gainsaying their utter nastiness.

Germaine Greer, feminist writer and academic

Listen, cats ladder your tights and so they must die.

Jenny Éclair, comedian

Sex and Other Laughing Matters

I can't understand why people throw sticks to dogs. Dogs aren't particularly interested in sticks, what they are interested in is crotches.

Jenny Éclair, comedian

I don't trust anyone. That's why I surround myself with animals. They can't talk.

Jordan, glamour model

I just heard on the radio yesterday that people are giving dogs Prozac. Well, there is a really good use of the gross national product. Cheering up dogs.

Fran Lebowitz, writer and humorist

A single woman with a dog is, somehow, nowhere near as tragic as one with a cat.

India Knight, journalist

Some people have surprise birthday parties for their dogs. That's just a waste, because any party would be a surprise to a dog.

Ellen DeGeneres, comedian

Don't accept your dog's admiration as conclusive evidence that you are wonderful.

Ann Landers, writer

When I see people wearing fur, I'm not sure if I should be chucking something at them or saying something. There's no good reason for wearing fur. And it even looks crap.

Sophie Ellis Bextor, pop singer

····· Miscellaneous ·············

What if? That's the dumbest thing in the world.

Elaine Stritch, actor

I read Shakespeare and the Bible, and I can shoot dice. That's what I call a liberal education.

Tallulah Bankhead, actor

I don't have pet peeves, I have whole kennels of irritation.

Whoopi Goldberg, comedian

I'm blonde, what's your excuse?

Reese Witherspoon, actor

Nutty as 12 monkeys in a 10 monkey barrel.

Daisy Donovan, TV presenter

Sex and Other Laughing Matters

I had a big collection of fried eggs that I painted.

Shakira, singer

I've been noticing gravity since I was very young.

Cameron Diaz, actor

Duct tape is like the force. It has a light side, a dark side, and it holds the universe together.

Oprah Winfrey, TV presenter

Cells let us walk, talk, think, make love and realise the bath water is cold.

Lorraine Lee Cudmore, scientist

There are certain people that are marked for death. I have my little list of those that treated me unfairly.

Jennifer Lopez, singer and actor

I spend a lot of my life in the back of cars – Oops! I didn't mean that in the way it sounded. Like, hence the two kids.

Kerry McFadden, pop singer

Man invented language to satisfy his deep need to complain.

Lily Tomlin, comedian

Miscellaneous

Did you ever walk in a room and forget why you walked in? I think that's how dogs spend their lives.

Sue Murphy, comedian

The problem with people who have no vices is that generally you can be pretty sure they're going to have some pretty annoying virtues.

Elizabeth Taylor, actor

Man may have discovered fire, but women discovered how to play with it.

Sarah Jessica Parker, actor

Streets without shops are my personal enemies.

Misia Sert, artist

I don't think about anything too much ... If I think too much, it kind of freaks me out.

Pamela Anderson, actor

The country is like a good woman abandoned for a bad woman – who is the town.

Caitlin Thomas, journalist

Sex and Other Laughing Matters

I always have a quotation for everything – it saves original thinking.

Dorothy L. Sayers, novelist

I like to drive with my knees. Otherwise, how can I put on my lipstick and talk on the phone?

Sharon Stone, actor

Nobody cares if you're miserable, so you might as well be happy.

Cynthia Nelms, writer

He who angers you conquers you.

Elizabeth Kenny, nurse

He has spectacularly lost his looks. He's turned into Princess Anne.

Feminist writer and academic Germaine Greer on Prince William

I might repeat to myself slowly and soothingly, a list of quotations beautiful from minds profound – if I can remember any of the damn things.

Dorothy Parker, writer and wit

A friend in need is a right pain in the arse.

Jenny Éclair, comedian

A friend will … threaten to kill anyone who tries to come into a room where you are trying on bathing suits.

Erma Bombeck, writer and humorist

I look for loyalty in my friends. That and returning phone calls.

Diane Modahl, athlete

I hope there's a tinge of disgrace about me. Hopefully, there's one good scandal left in me yet.

Diana Rigg, actor

A good listener is not someone who has nothing to say. A good listener is a good talker with a sore throat.

Katharine Whitehorn, journalist

The contents of a handbag, like good whiskey in a charred oak barrel, ripen and improve with age.

Peg Bracken, food writer

I like people who are pathological about things.

Zadie Smith, novelist

Sex and Other Laughing Matters

The only thing that scares me more than space aliens is the idea that there aren't any space aliens. We can't be the best creation has to offer.

Ellen DeGeneres, comedian

You know it's a bad day when you wake up and the birds are singing Leonard Cohen numbers.

Jenny Éclair, comedian

I don't clap. I'm busy.

Actor China Chow at the Los Angeles fashion week

You can tell the person who lives for others by the haunted look on the faces of the others.

Katherine Whitehorn, journalist

Time wounds all heels.

Jane Ace, radio entertainer

The trouble with trouble is that it all starts out as fun.

Naomi Judd, country and western singer

Forget psychiatry. Bottling It Up Is Best. Every time. So you die a little younger, what the hell? At least you get a bigger crowd at your funeral.

Maureen Lipman, actor

Between two evils, I always pick the one I never tried before.

Mae West, actor

Well, if I'm dysfunctional, who dysfuncted me?

Kathy Lette, writer

Advice is what we ask for when we already know the answer but wish we didn't.

Erica Jong, novelist

It's hard to be nice to some paranoid schizophrenic just because she lives in your body.

Judy Tenuta, comedian

I have a simple philosophy. Fill what's empty. Empty what's full, and scratch where it itches.

Alice Roosevelt Longworth, former American First Lady

If you can keep your head when all about you are losing theirs, it's quite possible you haven't grasped the situation.

Jean Kerr, playwright

Why do born-again people so often make you wish they'd never been born the first time?

Katherine Whitehorn, journalist

Sex and Other Laughing Matters

Now that we all travel abroad so much, there comes a dreadful moment in our lives when our foreign friends, whom we strongly urged to visit us, actually do so.

Virginia Graham, TV presenter

I wonder what the French say when they get déjà vu?

Hattie Hayridge, comedian

People would have more leisure time if it weren't for all the leisure time activities that use it up.

Peg Bracken, food writer

Say what you like about Genghis Kahn but, when he was around, old ladies could walk the streets of Mongolia at night.

Jo Brand, comedian

Life's a bitch and then they call you one.

Mary France Connelly, comedian

I have bursts of being a lady, but it doesn't last long.

Shelly Winters, actor

Writers are selfish people, with a love of their own company so passionate that it seems entirely likely that one day one of us just might get ourselves pregnant.

Julie Burchill, journalist

Oh God. I can't bear Sebastian Faulks. It's just Mills and Boon with guns!

Isabel Wolff, journalist

If women ruled the world and we all got massages, there would be no war.

Carrie Snow, comedian

The reason there are so few female politicians is that it is too much trouble to put make-up on two faces.

Maureen Murphy, actor

Neighbours? I'd rather have thrush.

Pamela Stephenson, actor

Many years ago we knew a girl who called herself a friend. She was so sweet that if you bit her you'd damage your teeth.

Alice Thomas Ellis, writer

Actions lie louder than words.

Carolyn Wells, writer

I hate to spread rumours – but what else can one do with them?

Amanda Lear, model-turned-singer

When someone walks down the aisle and says to you, 'Is someone sitting there?' just say, 'No one – except the Lord.'

Carol Leifer, writer and comedian

Jokes

Why did the Aussie bloke cross the road? 'Cause his dick was in the chicken.

Kathy Lette, writer

Boys, to put you at your ease, let me just say that at our all-girl gatherings, we don't just talk at length … We also talk about width.

Kathy Lette, writer

A comedian has to get a laugh from the audience, just the way a prostitute has to get an orgasm from the client.

Camille Paglia, academic

There is not one female comic who was a beautiful little girl.

Joan Rivers, comedian

He who laughs last didn't get it.

Helen Giangregorio, writer

Why do little boys whine? Because they are practising to be men.

Anonymous

Mary had a little lamb and the doctor fainted.

Anonymous

Why is psychoanalysis a lot quicker for men than for women? When it's time to go back to his childhood, he's already there.

Anonymous

Instant gratification is not soon enough.

Meryl Streep, actor

Sex and Other Laughing Matters

Computer dating: it's terrific if you're a computer.

Rita Mae Brown, writer

I thought *coq au vin* was love in a lorry.

Victoria Wood, comedian

Why is it good that there are female astronauts?
Because when the crew gets lost in space, at least
the women will ask for directions.

Anonymous

Not only is life a bitch, it has puppies.

Adrienne E. Gusoff, teacher and writer

Things are always darkest just before they go pitch
black.

Kelly Robinson, writer

If brevity is the soul of wit, your penis must be a
riot.

Donna Gephart, journalist

If they can put a man on the moon ... why can't
they put them all there?

Anonymous

This guy says, 'I'm perfect for you, because I'm a cross between a macho and a sensitive man.' I said, 'Oh, a gay trucker?'

Judy Tenuta, comedian

Index

Index

Index

Index

Index

Sarandon, Susan 26, 159
Sargent, Claire 144
Saunders, Jennifer 31, 32,
    121, 150
Sayers, Dorothy L. 89, 202
Schaffer, Zenna 130
Schiaparelli, Elsa 36
Schmich, Mary 42
Schwarzenegger, Arnold 67
Scott, Liz 88
Segal, Naomi 59
Sert, Misia 201
sex 167–74
Shakespeare, William 142
Shakira 140, 190, 200
Shepherd, Cybill 112
Shields, Carol 137
Silverstone, Alicia 106
Simpson, Bart 102
Simpson, Marge 102
Skinner, Cornleia Otis 77
Smith, Ali 115
Smith, Anna Nicole 177
Smith, Bessie 59
Smith, Patti 65
Smith, Stevie 168
Smith, Tracy 177
Smith, Zadie 203
Snow, Carrie 160, 207
Solanas, Valerie 66
Sonique 24
Spark, Muriel 159, 167
Spears, Britney 25, 34, 152
Speed 136
sport 129–30
Stanwyck, Barbara 108
Stark, Freya 73

Stasi, Linda 152
status 141–4
Steel, Dawn 91
Stefani, Gwen 30, 34
Stein, Gertrude 118, 142
Steinem, Gloria 43, 118, 142,
    188, 195
Stephenson, Pamela 81, 207
Stern, Judith 19
Stevenson, Helen 90
Stewart, Martha 138
Stewart, Rod 95
Sting 102
Stinnett, Caskie 118
Stirling, Rachel 22
Stone, Sharon 112, 143, 176,
    202
Streep, Meryl 101, 209
Streisand, Barbra 104, 187
Stritch, Elaine 199
success 89–92
Swanson, Gloria 122, 135

T

Tandy, Jessica 181
Tartt, Donna 122
Taylor, Elizabeth 56, 70, 137,
    141, 201
technology 92–4
Temple, Shirley 110
Tenuta, Judy 27, 158, 175,
    205, 211
Thatcher, Margaret 45, 46, 72,
    88, 117, 118, 119, 142
Thirkell, Angela 98

Index